THE COMPLETE POTTER:

POTS FOR PLANTS AND GARDENS

THE COMPLETE POTTER:

POTS FOR PLANTS AND GARDENS

JOHN HUGGINS

SERIES EDITOR EMMANUEL COOPER

B. T. Batsford Ltd, London

ISBN 0 7134 62841

Typeset by Servis Filmsetting Ltd,
Manchester
and printed in Hong Kong
for the publishers
B. T. Batsford Ltd
4 Fitzhardinge Street
London W1H 0AH

*The front cover shows a pedestal pot in
terracotta, by Stephen Dixon*

CONTENTS

Introduction   7

1 Clay and Its Preparation   10

2 Throwing   15

3 Press Moulding   30

4 Machine-Assisted Production   40

5 Handbuilding   42

6 Design and Decoration   48

7 Drying and Firing   66

8 Weather Resistance   71

9 Plants for Pots   77

10 Decorative Bricks, Tiles and Other Ornaments   81

Suppliers   93

Index   94

INTRODUCTION

A simple terracotta pot brims with geraniums in their prime, scarlet clusters gently swaying above sculptured lobes of variegated green. Below, tucked against the warm red rim, cushions of blue lobelia are spiked with brilliant white eyes.

Where shall we put this pot? Placed in a dull corner of the garden, that area comes to life, as if a spotlight had been turned on. Stood at the end of a path or view, perhaps on a brick pedestal or wooden stump, it becomes a focal point, a colourful full stop at the end of the vista. Place it by a seat on a patio or lawn and it will add delight to those relaxed moments. A pair of such pots put on either side of the front door will add both colour and formality to the entrance. Perhaps we might bring it indoors and stand it, just for the day, in the middle of the kitchen table!

Plant pots bring versatility and convenience to gardening as well as style and interest. A box hedge planted in the open ground is a fixture, part of a permanent garden design. A collection of box plants in pots, however, is a movable feature: one day they may be placed in a straight formal line dividing one part of a patio from another, the next they may be divided into informal groups, perhaps acting as foils to pots of colourful annuals.

Pots of plants come and go with the seasons. Since pots are movable, if not by hand then with the help of a trolley, they can be brought into prominence as the plants come into their prime, then later, when the plants are past their best, they may be retired into a greenhouse or a less prominent part of the garden. Pots full of crocuses may be replaced by tubs of daffodils or tulips. Summer-flowering annuals may then replace the bulbs, in either the same or alternative pots. As the summer flowers fade, pots of autumn-flowering chrysanthemums may be brought forward to replace them while these, in turn, may be superseded by pots of variegated ivy or by dwarf conifers under-planted with bulbs waiting to herald the first signs of the following spring.

The labour involved in planting and maintaining groups of pots is minimal in comparison with that involved with more extensive gardening. Even when seasonal bulbs and annuals are planted, the labour involved is far less than in preparing and planting out open beds. For even greater convenience and less maintenance, pots may be planted to give year-long interest with flowering shrubs or small trees under-planted with evergreen foliage plants.

Pots can play an important role in garden design, particularly in the smaller gardens and patios so common today. They also offer convenience and flexibility, providing a method of gardening attractive to people who do not have the time or inclination to prepare, plant, weed, and maintain large beds of plants.

Besides their function as containers for plants, garden pots are also valued as pots in their own right, products of the potter's art. A good pot combines various qualities of design, balance, feel, presence, and energy that may be appreciated without any reference to gardens or siting at all. A good pot that is a good garden pot, however, is at its best when sited in a garden or paved patio where it can be seen in relation to other architectural materials and plant forms. A good pot will draw attention and give

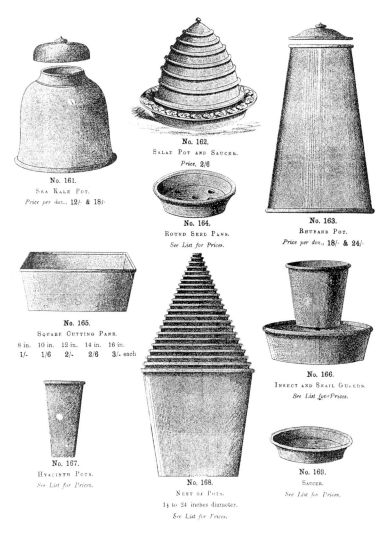

No. 161.
Sea Kale Pot.
Price per doz., 12/- & 18/-

No. 162.
Salad Pot and Saucer.
Price, 2/6

No. 164.
Round Seed Pans.
See List for Prices.

No. 163.
Rhubarb Pot.
Price per doz., 18/- & 24/-

No. 165.
Square Cutting Pans.

8 in.	10 in.	12 in.	14 in.	16 in.
1/-	1/6	2/-	2/6	3/- each

No. 167.
Hyacinth Pots.
See List for Prices.

No. 168.
Nest of Pots.
1½ to 24 inches diameter.
See List for Prices.

No. 166.
Insect and Snail Guards.
See List for Prices.

No. 169.
Saucer.
See List for Prices.

pleasure when empty, but will not draw undue attention when planted. Usually a pot plays a supporting role when its contents are in their prime and drawing all attention. A pot that is too busy in its design and loud in presence draws attention away from the plants it supports and will quickly wear out its welcome in the garden. Occasionally, however, roles are reversed and plants play a supporting role to a dramatic or otherwise elaborate pot. Some garden pots are not intended to be planted, but stand as pieces of sculpture. Their mass and form are attractions in a garden setting, their sense of stillness and drama often gaining depth by the constant shifting of breeze-blown foliage.

Page from catalogue of the Royal Potteries of Weston-super-Mare. Courtesy Woodspring Museum

Besides functional and sculptural pots other clay works come into the category of garden ornaments. Decorative wall panels, tiles, statuary, and sundials can be included here, and the category extended to cover edging tiles, paving, and coping bricks.

Part of the appeal of a good handmade plant pot lies in the way the chosen materials and the method of making combine to produce a pot that looks at home in a garden, a pot that is in sympathy with its environment. A pot that has been machined (and there are plenty about) is conspicuously smooth and hard-edged, standing out rather than mellowing in. Slip casting is similarly inappropriate for garden pots: the pot wall is inevitably thin, the surface too smooth, and the technique encourages manufacturers to produce designs that are excessively detailed.

In the following chapters this book will range across various methods of making pots for plants and gardens as used by individual craftspeople and small workshops. Terracotta is the clay most commonly used for plant pots, both historically and today, and this is reflected in the book. Other clays, notably stoneware, also have their place.

Rather than devoting a chapter to the history of country potteries specializing in plant pots, I have included references to them in various chapters where appropriate. Suffice it to say that small country potteries flourished throughout England during the late eighteenth century, producing ranges of plain and slip-decorated domestic wares from local deposits of clay. Plant pot making was related to this production, but was also often an extension of brick making, and both activities were seasonal. As the popularity of gardening grew in the mid-nineteenth century and nurseries developed to satisfy the demand for plants, so the market for plant pots grew. The production of plant pots was in its heyday from the mid-nineteenth century until the First World War, and numerous potteries grew into substantial businesses during this period. Some potteries were revived after the war, but very few managed to continue beyond the Second World War. The production of the plastic flower pot, coupled with the attractions for staff of working in new light industries, dealt a death blow to the traditional production of terracotta plant pots.

Times have changed and the demand for plant pots of all sorts is increasing. Plastics have lost their novelty and most people agree that a plastic pot is a hideous sight in a garden. People have learned that plastic fades and becomes brittle, and that whereas the beauty of a clay pot increases with age and even chipped and cracked pots have their charm, old plastic shivers into unsightly strips blown into corners and under hedging. Today there is a growing interest in developing the garden and in treating it as an extra room beyond the house. Just as the interior rooms require furnishing to make them attractive, so the garden should be well furnished too. This growing market is largely being catered for by the accompanying spread of garden centres. Generally, such centres pander their mass market with a mass product. Their criteria is not the quality of the pots they stock, but simply the number of tons of pots that they can sell. The interest in gardens and pots for gardens is, however, widespread and there is a growing number of discerning people prepared to pay more for pots of better quality and individuality.

CHAPTER ONE

CLAY AND ITS PREPARATION

Adequate and appropriate preparation of the clay is important for all methods of clay work. In the case of throwing it is essential. Not all terracotta clays are alike and in order to throw large terracotta pots well, it is necessary to choose a clay that is fit for the job.

Such a clay must be highly plastic and able to be worked while soft. The mass of clay on the wheel must be soft enough to readjust easily under pressure during centring, be thrown without undue exertion, and stay where it is put without sagging. Small pots need to be lifted from the wheel without distorting, while other pots need finishing with decoration or, as in the case of herb pots, need holes pierced in their sides while still on the wheel. If the clay cannot support itself during these operations, then even small pots have to be thrown on bats and all finishing needs to wait until the clay has hardened off a little. Lifting a day's production of large herb pots down from the shelves simply to cut holes in them expends a lot of extra time and effort.

My own experience of trying to throw large terracotta plant pots with commercially available clays from Stoke-on-Trent was devastating. I could throw pots that were reasonably large only if the clay was fairly hard. In order to throw the pots I had to break my back and exhaust my wrists. If I made the clay soft, it was easy to centre and open, but repeated lifts to thin and raise the walls ended in frustrated disappointment as the clay walls sagged: instead of growing taller, the pots became shorter. I was reduced to despair.

I tried adding various grogs and sands to coarsen the clay, but found this was of limited benefit. Although a good matrix of various sizes of non-clay materials wedged into a clay will help it stand firm, it is the bonding of the clay particles that gives the body its strength. I reached the point where I was adding such a high proportion of sand and grog that when I packed the dry pots into the kiln a large number of them cracked. A slight knock or the weight of one pot resting on another was sufficient to break the body, made too brittle by the reduced level of clay material.

It is worth remembering that the decline of the country potteries, each sited on their own source of clay, was balanced by, and in part caused by, the rise of industrialized pottery making around Stoke-on-Trent. Industrial pottery making became established on the site of Etruria Marls because the clay was so appropriate for industrial methods: it could be worked in a much stiffer state than the sticky clays of the country potteries. It could be pressed, jiggered, and jollied into shape – in short, bullied – by machines and mechanical power. For such industrial processes the highly plastic clays of the country workshops were useless. Today people have forgotten this and try to throw big ware with the less plastic bodies based on Etruria Marls.

Plasticity in clay is ultimately due to the particle size of the clay: the finer the particle the more plastic the clay. It also follows that the smaller the particle the greater the bond between the particles. This means that a highly plastic clay will accept a high addition of sand or grog without losing its strength and will tolerate considerable softening with water without sagging during throwing. Although it is particle size that governs plasticity, it is water that lubricates the particles, enabling them to move under pressure. A good throwing clay will have a water content of about 25–30 per cent.

Terracotta clays are common throughout large areas of Britain and many are highly plastic. Brickyards often mark the existence of such deposits, although the number of small brickyards has declined rapidly since the Second World War. Some deposits of terracotta clay are clean and workable when dug up and require only rudimentary preparation before being ready to throw.

Traditionally, brick making and pot making were seasonal occupations. The clay was dug in the autumn and spread over a wide area about 1m (3ft) deep. When the frosts and rain had broken down the clay it was turned with spades two or three times. In smaller workshops it was then treaded by feet into a workable consistency, while bigger workshops had a pugmill worked by a horse or donkey. The clay was fed into the top of the cylinder to be cut up by blades rotating at right angles to the shaft before being pushed out at the other end.

Today this simple technique can be copied but on a shorter time scale. Spread the rough clay about 23cm (9in) deep on a concrete bed and spray it with water. The next day turn the clay with a spade and add more water if necessary. The following day the clay should be soft enough to put through the pugmill. I used to prepare half a ton at a time by this method. If you encounter any stones during preparation, simply lift them out. Even when the clay is on the wheel it is not too late to remove stones. I have watched an old potter stop halfway through making a pot to pick out a large stone from the pot wall and throw it into a corner. The stone left a hole like a window right through the pot. A piece of clay torn from the next ball was quickly modelled into the hole and smoothed over inside and out, and the throwing completed, just as a gardener lifts away a stone that has surfaced in the seedbed.

It is a lucky potter who finds a source of sufficiently clean clay. Most clays need to be cleaned of roots and stones before they are ready to be thrown. Some clays are cleaned adequately by grinding into small pieces and crushing impurities to a size where they are not such a problem. Pan grinders, roller mills, and jaw crushers can all be used with varying degrees of success, but such machines are really more appropriate for clay that is to be used for bricks, rather than thrown on a wheel; a pebble can be crushed into an army of tiny razor-sharp pieces.

Another common impurity and arch enemy of the potter is lime. This can occur as chalk seams running through a clay bed or as fossil material scattered throughout a clay deposit. Such impurities, if they are small, do not matter much during the making processes and are not apparent even when the kiln is opened. If there are pieces of lime in the pot walls, however, they will have been turned into hydrated lime in the kiln and will now suck up moisture. As the lime absorbs moisture through the clay wall, it expands and bursts its way out, often breaking a large flake of clay away from the side of the pot or a big chunk out of the rim. Depending on the amount of moisture in the atmosphere, this process can take several weeks to complete, by which time the pot could be sitting in a shop or gallery. If lime is known to be present in a clay which is to be used for potting, the addition of common salt to the clay can help reduce the number and severity of lime blows. Alternatively, all pots from the kiln can be soaked in baths of water for a few hours to make sure that any that are going to suffer blows will do so before they are sold.

The most thorough and satisfactory method of cleaning clay is to turn it into a slip and sieve out all unwanted material. To do this the clay, or the various clays if more than one is being mixed, is dug into a blunger partially filled with water. The blades of the blunger race round, mixing the clay and water to a slip, creating sound effects similar to Niagara Falls. Our clay takes about three hours to blunge thoroughly, after which it is pumped through an old sludge pump into a vibratory sieve. All grit, roots, lime, and other unwanted material are removed as the slip passes through the sieve and into the holding ark. From the ark the slip is then pumped into the filter press.

The filter press is a row of cast iron plates

each having a recessed area around a central hole. The plates slide to open or close on bars, one each side. One end plate is solid and is called the king plate. The other end plate is fixed and has a hole through which the slip is pumped; this end is called the queen plate. When the press is closed up, it is held together by four tie bars, securely tightened by huge nuts. Between the cast iron plates of the press are two pairs of cloths made of non-rotting man-made fibres. The inner cloths are of a fine weave that allows water through, but not clay particles. The backing cloths are made of a coarser material with a fairly open weave. The slip is pumped into the press under pressure, either from a hydraulic pump or, as in our case, an old deadweight pump. Once the press is full and the pressure has climbed to 827.4kPa (120 psi), the water is forced out of the slip and, over the next few hours, the cakes of plastic clay are formed.

Unfortunately, highly plastic clays do not like being filter pressed. As the pressure builds up, the fine particles are forced against the cloths, to form a skin which in turn restricts the passage of the water. Consequently, highly plastic clays, such as ball clays and good terracottas, need to stay in the press under pressure for several hours, in our case about ten hours. If we did not add sand at the slip stage, the pressing would take even longer. (In contrast, the less plastic terracotta bodies based on Etruria Marls from Stoke-on-Trent are fully pressed within

Clay preparation equipment: blunger, ark, and sludge pump

Filter press and pugmill

three hours.) Once the pressing is over and the clay is hard enough, the press is opened and the clay cakes dropped out ready for pugging. Because of skin formed by the fine clay particles, the cakes tend to be much softer on the inside than the outside. If the clay is pugged through a shredder plate and a de-airing chamber, it is ready to throw after going through the pug once. If the pugmill has only a single chamber, the clay needs to be pugged twice, preferably leaving it overnight between puggings.

De-airing clay with a vacuum pump attached to the pug sucks air bubbles out of the body and brings the clay particles into closer contact. This process increases the workability of the clay, but it also makes it more dense. This means that centring is harder and irregularities occurring during throwing are harder to iron out. This is another reason why commercially prepared clays are less satisfactory for throwing big ware. Pugging is easiest when a strong vacuum pump helps pull the clay through the first chamber and fully de-airs the clay when it enters the second barrel. When preparing our clay we adjust the vacuum pump to be strong enough to help pull the clay through the pug, but not so strong that the pugged clay is too dense for us to enjoy working it.

Although the thumb test will give a good idea of the hardness or softness of a prepared clay, a more accurate measure is given by a penetrometer. This is a small stainless steel instrument with a spring-loaded point that is pushed into the clay. Each different clay has an optimum water content, but ours works best when the penetrometer reads between 3.5 to 5 on a scale going up to 10.

The advantage of using the filter press method for cleaning clay is that it removes all unwanted materials with the minimum of effort. Different clays can be thoroughly blended in the blunger along with fine sands or other non-clay materials. Any sands or grogs that are too large to go through the sieve must be added into the ark or into the pugmill. The disadvantage of this method is that it requires considerable space and machinery. Another factor is that, even when the volumes of the various clays and sands going into the blunger are constant and the pint weight of the slip checked, the consistency of the clay cakes coming from the press varies widely between pressings. The season appears to affect the time needed to press up the clay: summer pressings can be several hours shorter than winter ones.

Samples of clay, or small batches, can be prepared without the need for any machinery at all. Dig a few spadefuls of clay from the garden, or from a deposit that looks promising, and leave the material to dry either in the open or indoors near a source of heat. When it is dry break up any big lumps with a hammer and drop the pebble-sized pieces into a series of buckets, or a dustbin half-filled with water. If the clay is thoroughly dry it will quickly break down in the water; leather-hard pieces will resist the water's penetration. Give the mix a stir and leave overnight for the water to do its work.

Next day get your hands into the buckets and mix the clay and water into a slurry. If the mixture is thick add more water. If there are any hard lumps try and squeeze them between your fingers. If the mixture feels too lumpy leave it for another day, stirring and squeezing occasionally. When the mixture is of a fairly even slip consistency pour it through a sieve, using a stiff washing up bowl to persuade it. A 30 or 40 mesh sieve is quite adequate: an 80 mesh will remove all tooth.

When you have collected one or more buckets of the sieved slip you will then need to remove the moisture to bring the clay to the plastic state. If a half-full bucket is simply left to stand in a warm room for a few weeks the clay will dry to a plastic state, but the process will be much quicker if the slip is poured into wooden fruit boxes lined with hessian or a piece of old sheet. You could try hanging the slip in an old pillow case or other finely woven sack. Either way, with sufficient heat and air movement, the clay will soon be stiff enough to wedge and get on to the wheel.

Many surface clays used for plant pots suffer from the presence of soluble salts. These are not noticeable in the raw clay, but migrate to the surface during drying, to form a thin layer of crystals on the surface. When the kiln door is opened, instead of a bank of bright terracotta pots, all the surfaces are covered with an unsightly white scum. Where the crystals have been broken during handling before firing, a permanent record of white finger prints become visible on the fired pots. Fortunately it is easy to prevent the soluble salts appearing. An addition of up to 0.3 per cent barium carbonate to the clay will fix the salts and the pots will come clean and bright from the kiln.

Highly plastic clays have a high shrinkage. Adding sand helps to open the body up and lessen the shrinkage, while at the same time adding tooth to the clay. It is better to add a variety of grain sizes when opening up a body rather than simply adding quantities of very coarse material. The matrix created by a variety of particle sizes is much stronger than a mixture of very fine and very coarse. In fact, a clay that is prone to cracking during drying may benefit as much from additions of clay of medium to low plasticity as from additions of sand or grog.

CHAPTER TWO

THROWING

For most small potteries producing plant pots in quantity, wheel-thrown work constitutes the bulk of production. The wheel, powered either by a swinging leg or by electricity, provides the potter with a versatile and efficient tool. With neither bulky plastic moulds nor heavy pressing machinery, potters combine their skill with the thrust of the spinning wheel. Muscle, eye, and sensitivity co-ordinate to produce hollow pots from solid balls of clay. A skilled thrower is able to produce considerable quantities of pots in a day's production, their dimensions constant to within a few millimetres, yet no two identical. However many are made, each pot carries the impression of the moment, and the unstamped imprint of its maker, flowing generously with the relaxed spirit of a contented mind, or tight and mean when anxieties intrude.

It is this ability of the spinning clay to respond to changes in finger pressure and to the changing positions of body, hands, and fingers that makes the wheel such a versatile tool. If throwers want to change the dimensions or even shape of a pot they can

do so at once. No lengthy preparation is needed making master models and working moulds.

It is, however, this immediate response to varying pressure that makes working the wheel a hard task. A good, well-thrown pot is made with the minimum number of movements, its freshness reflecting the professional directness of the maker. The length of time a piece of clay is spinning on the wheel is very short, even for large pots. Throwers must, therefore, be prepared and concentrate – they must centre their mind before they can centre the clay. As the production run gets under way and the pots begin to flow, so the thrower begins to relax and movement becomes more fluid. Although the moves made by body and hands appear the same, the mind, while alert, becomes free. The flowing rise and fall of the clay and the swelling of the form are like a dance, the repeated moves of body and hand marking out the rhythm.

Some people find throwing tedious once they have mastered the basic techniques, but I have always found it a considerable source of

pleasure, and a challenge. Once a particular shape or weight of clay is mastered, the challenge of a new shape, technique, or weight of clay appears. I sometimes think that I continue to enjoy throwing because I do not find it easy. Traditionally the apprenticeship for a thrower in the country potteries was seven years. In some cases apprentices had to graduate through weighing up clay and carrying wareboards to turning the slave wheel of a master potter before they could begin to throw pots at all.

TECHNIQUES

The basic stages of centring, opening up, and lifting the clay are the same whether the lump of clay is small or large. Small plant pots that will fire to about 15cm (6in) in height require a ball of clay weighing 1.8–2kg (4–5lb). A pot much larger than 15cm (6in) can of course be made from such a weight of clay, but it would be too thin to be appropriate for a garden.

The ball of clay is thrown on to the centre of the wheel and splashed with water. With the wheel spinning fast, the clay is centred with pressure from the left palm aided with pressure from the right-hand fingers on the opposite side. Irregularities in the clay are pushed out at the top of the spinning cone. The clay cone is then flattened with the outside edge of the right hand, which then turns over and opens up the clay with pressure from the balls of the fingers, especially the middle finger. The drainage hole is made simultaneously as the base is opened out.

The clay wall is then squeezed inwards and upwards between the palm of the left hand on the outside and the fingers of the right hand inside. The movement is finished with a firm finger held on the rim to keep it thick

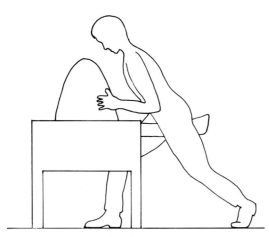

Body positioned for throwing

and regular. This will have achieved half the height while the rest will be made by a single lift of the clay in the usual manner on the right-hand side of the pot. Be sure to keep the inside fingers ahead of those on the outside and to thicken the rim again with a firm finger. The pot will now be in the standard cooling tower shape and all that is now required is to give the pot its final shape by running the fingers of the left hand up the inside wall, applying pressure where needed, while simultaneously running a wooden rib up the outside wall to remove excessive throwing rings and any slippery slurry.

The base is then trimmed with a pointed rib and the pot wired off the wheel head. With reasonably dry hands there should be no trouble lifting a pot this size off the wheel and on to the ware board.

However, when larger weights of clay are thrown it is necessary to adapt one's technique in order to move the mass of clay on the wheel without wasting energy. The larger the lump of clay, the more the thrower must use the weight and structure of his entire body rather than relying on over-worked fingers. I have watched throwers who are extremely competent at making small domestic pots finding it difficult to come to terms with larger balls of clay because they would not accept that they needed to learn new ways of handling the clay.

The skill of throwing is based on a balance between rigidity and sensitivity. The thrower must be sufficiently firm and unbending,

especially during centring, to impose his will on the clay. At the same time, but especially during the later stages of throwing, he must be sensitive to vagaries in the clay, alert to whether the fingers need more or less pressure, whether the wheel is at the right speed, and whether the clay is sufficiently lubricated. Large pots take a lot of energy to throw, so when large numbers have to be made, it is important to prepare the clay and oneself carefully. An American potter has said, 'If you can lift it, you can throw it'. Personally, I am happy throwing 20kg (45lb) of clay at a time and will throw 27kg (60lb) if it is necessary, though I prefer not to. Pots requiring more clay are best made in two or more stages (see page 22).

KNEADING

The prepared clay should be kneaded ready to place on the wheel to ensure that any slight hardening of the clay surface during storage is thoroughly mixed in with the softer clay. Kneading also brings the particles of clay into a spiral pattern that may assist with the throwing. In order not to wear oneself out, it is a good idea to knead several small weights of clay rather than one large mass. For a 20kg (45lb) pot I weigh out two pieces of 9kg (20lb) and one of 2kg (5lb). As I finish kneading the clay I form it into different shapes: the first large lump into a flattish pancake, the second into an oval cone, and the small piece into a little cone. When these shapes are assembled on the wheel they are already in a cone shape and therefore require less effort centring. With the wheel spinning, I beat them with my hands to join the three masses together and to bring them as near the centre as possible.

CENTRING

With the wheel spinning fast and the clay well lubricated with water, the centring of the mass is achieved primarily by locking my left elbow into my hip and leaning against the clay. My fingers are not used much, but the fleshy part of my palm is used like a pad on the end of a straight lever (my arm). Sometimes I stretch my left leg behind to provide extra support. The purpose of this is

to use my bodyweight and the structure of my anatomy to iron out any unevenness in the clay and coax it into the centre, rather than using muscle and physical energy. I push upwards and then downwards on the cone, sometimes finding it helpful to trim away uneven clay from the bottom, using the index finger of my right hand as a blade. It is important that the mass of clay is fairly well centred before proceeding, although firm direct handling throughout the throwing will persuade minor irregularities back in line.

Driving the hole down the centre of the clay is one of the more dramatic moments of throwing large pots. I sink a dish shape into the top of the cone with the palm of my right hand, then make a cup-shaped depression in this with the massed fingers of the right hand. I then fill this depression with water, ready to lubricate the clay as the hole is made. Standing up over the wheel head I clench my right fist with the knuckle of the middle finger protruding then drive this down through the mass of the spinning clay, right down to the wheel head. Provided there is sufficient water to keep fist and clay lubricated, the hole is easily made.

OPENING UP

Opening up the base of the pot is the next procedure, and this is done while leaving the coned mass undisturbed. The last thing one wants is for the mass of clay to be pulled back in order to complete the base, only to be pushed back in again for the lifting of the

Clay balls assembled to form a cone

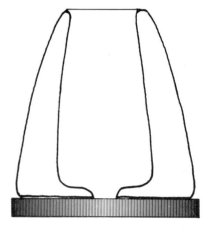

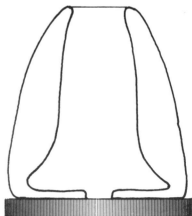

Section through tall clay hump showing base opened up

clay. With the fingers of my right hand massed like a mole's paw, and using my left hand to steady it, the base of the pot is widened, undercutting the mass of clay. Although it is not possible to get callipers down there to ensure the base is open sufficiently for the size of the pot, it is possible to use a throwing rib to gauge the distance from the clay wall to the centre. Once the base is wide enough and the centre drainage hole tidy, it is time to start lifting the clay in the walls.

LIFTING

To begin lifting the clay I work on the left of the mass as during centring. This makes maximum use of the force of the clay revolving against a buttressed palm. Supporting the clay wall on the inside with my right hand, the palm of my left hand is driven up the side of the wall with a steady piston-like movement, increasing its height and thinning it at the same time. I repeat this procedure a further once or twice, taking care to fatten down the rim after each lift. By the end of the third lift on the left of the pot the walls are quite high and still in the standard cooling-tower shape. Switching to the right-hand side I press my forefinger hard down on the rim until it is really thick, while at the same time pulling the rim outwards.

Beating with hands to join the masses of clay together

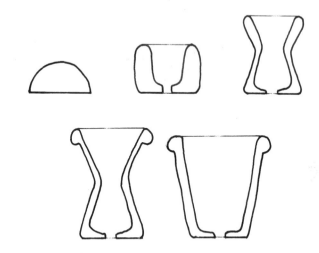

Stages in the throwing of a simple flowerpot

Driving the hole down the centre of the clay

Lifting

Using the sponge

Fattening the rim

Spongeing out excess water

I then lift the clay on the right side in the usual way, straightening the wall out as I go. I like to throw with a piece of wet sponge between my index finger and the pot as this helps to lubricate the wall and spread the pressure. Having reached the top I again fatten the rim and lean it out almost to its full width, then make the final lift, thinning and raising the clay wall for the last time. A final sweep with the fingers, applying pressure on the inside of the pot, ensures that the form is generous.

Clean up the pot by cutting away with a pointed rib any excess clay around the base,

before skimming a flat rib over the surface to minimize throwing ridges and to remove excess slurry. I then sponge water out of the pot, and run the sponge up the inside of the pot: there is enough water in the clay itself to dry out, without putting the pot aside dripping.

There is great pleasure and satisfaction in throwing big pots and dealing with large masses of clay. In order to avoid pains, strains, and exhaustion it is important that the clay is soft and that the weight and structure of the whole body are used, not just the muscles.

Pots that need to be made from a weight of clay greater than the thrower is happy to handle in one piece are best made in two or more parts. This can best be done by either of two methods: throwing and joining, or throwing and coiling. I prefer the former because it is quicker, although for very wide pots the second method might be more suitable.

Since both methods involve re-positioning pots on the wheel head, it is advisable to have thick lugs protruding from the wheel head matched with holes in the throwing bats.

Matching the pot's dimensions using callipers

Positioning the new pot on the original

THROWING AND JOINING

The lower part of the pot is first thrown in the usual way, finishing off with a fairly wide but not overhanging thickness at the top. The pot is then put aside to harden off, though I like to lay strips of polythene on the rim to keep that part soft. By the next day the base is usually firm enough and the internal diameter is measured with callipers. A fresh ball of clay, usually weighing rather less than the first pot, is now thrown on a bat into a bottomless pot. The clay wall is left thick and the rim pulled out to match the dimensions of the callipers. Before lifting the pot aside it is necessary to score the surface of the rim ready to join it to the base pot.

The original pot is then re-positioned on the wheel head and its rim scored. It is a good idea to smear sticky slurry over the scored rim to ensure a good join, but if the clay is sufficiently soft, this is not essential.

Pinching and twisting the clay together

Beating the join with a butter pat

Throwing again

The fresh bottomless pot is now lifted up, turned over, and placed carefully on top of the original pot. The clay of the two pots is now pinched together, with the thumb and first finger dug well into the clay of each part. At the same time as being pinched, the clay should be twisted in an effort to really marry the clay of the two rims. Once the pinching is complete all round the rim the bat is wired away from the pot, taking care that the wire stays flat on the bat. With the bat removed it is now possible to go round the inside seam and repeat the pinching there. When that is completed, the join on the outside should then be beaten all round with a butter pat, while the inside is supported with the left hand. This beating helps to flatten the pinches out and to double-check that the two pots are thoroughly joined. The inner seam is then worked over with a rib, smoothing off and filling in.

Now the two pots are inseparably joined, throwing can begin again. I start by trueing up the thick rim and opening it out, then throwing, on the right of the pot, from the join upwards. Usually two lifts are enough to thin the wall and gain the required height. I use a flat-edged rib to clean up the join area on the outside and a curved rib to do the same inside the pot. A last sweep with the fingers, applying pressure on the inside, gives the pot its final form. A variation on this

Svend Bayer throwing and coiling 48cm (19in) plant pots. Beating the clay

technique, traditional in Sussex potteries at the turn of the century, was to cut a wide groove in the rim of the bottom pot and to finish the rim of the second pot with a ridge fashioned with a square tool. When the two pots were joined together, the ridge fitted easily into the groove and ensured that with sufficient beating the clay from the two parts were adequately mixed together.

Certain pots, such as chimney pots and rhubarb forcers, may be made in two or more

parts and assembled straight away without waiting for the lower parts to harden off. Because of their shape – broad at the base and narrow at the top – the walls of the lower parts are structurally able to support the upper weight of clay without bowing and buckling.

A variation on this method of making two-part pots is to throw the top part of the pot the right way up, but without a base. The base of the top part is measured across the outside with callipers and put aside. The base part is then thrown with the outside rim to the measure of the callipers. When the rim of the top part is sufficiently hard to be handled without distorting, the pot is wired off and placed carefully on the scored rim of the base pot. The join is then treated in the same way as previously described. This method is fine so long as the two parts match adequately, but since the top is now too hard to throw, no further shaping can be done.

THROWING AND COILING

Svend Bayer makes a range of stoneware plant pots using the throw and coil technique. By this method he makes pots up to 66cm (26in) high by 56cm (22in) across. He sited his workshop close by his chosen source of clay and began by preparing it himself. Choosing to work entirely alone, he found that as the demand for his pots grew, it was easier and more economical to concentrate on throwing pots, letting someone else

prepare the clay. The rough clay is now transported from the pit in Devon up to Stoke-on-Trent where it is cleaned and processed, then transported back to Devon in convenient 25kg (55lb) bags. His clay body is highly plastic and finely toothed, a simple mixture of 70 per cent ball clay and 30 per cent grog.

Svend Bayer's 48cm (19in) plant pot is made in three stages. He starts with a 13.6kg (30lb) ball of clay and beats it with his palms into an even disc as near the centre of the wheel as possible. Then, instead of pitting his strength against the spinning mass of clay in the usual way of centring, he beats into the clay with his fist to hollow the lump into a thick-walled bowl. Care has to be taken to ensure the base is evenly and sufficiently thick and that the wall of clay is as uniform as possible. The base is not opened out all the way until the throwing proper begins. Once the beating is done, the clay wall is well lubricated with water and the thick ring of clay centred. Centring a ring of clay requires far less effort than working a mass of clay. The bottom part of the pot is then thrown in the usual way until the wall is quite thin. He takes care that the rim is even and, rather than fattening it up, leaves it quite thin and almost pointed. The pot is then put aside to harden.

When the base is firm enough, usually the next day, the pot is returned to the wheel.

Laying on a coil of clay

Svend Bayer spends some time making sure the base pot is still true and scrapes away any unevenness as the wheel turns, paying attention again to the fairly sharp pointed rim. Taking one of a batch of carefully weighed and rolled coils of clay, he lays it on the rim of the pot, squeezing it down over the rim and thinning it as he goes. The coil of 3.4kg (7½lb) is just sufficient to go round the rim. Supporting the clay wall on the inside, Svend Bayer then squeezes the coil with the palm of his right hand on the outside. Working with a quick, steady rhythm he secures the clay from the coil on the clay of the base pot, both inside and out, and thins the coil as the height grows. After squeezing with his hands, Svend Bayer then uses a tool to smooth away irregularities. The wall of clay is deliberately made to lean inwards at this stage. When that coil is sufficiently thinned and true, a second coil is added and the process repeated. When the second coil has been satisfactorily thinned and the pot wall grown sufficiently, the clay is then lubricated with water and the clay wall made true in the usual manner of throwing. The clay is not lifted during this process, simply trued up and smoothed and drawn out from its inward leaning shape. When this stage is finished, the pot is then put aside to harden.

When the pot is again firm enough to accept more coils, it is lifted back onto the wheel. This time, with the wheel moving slowly, Svend Bayer works over the surface of the pot with a large wooden paddle, ironing out any unevennesses that may have appeared and, again, paying particular attention to the rim. As with the middle section, a 3.4kg (7½lb) coil is laid on the rim, squeezed to the required height and scraped to ensure a reasonably smooth surface. The final coil is added to form the thick rim, rather than to gain additional height. Rather than being laid on the existing rim, it is laid beside it, then tooled into the clay from the previous coil. Finally, water is added to enable the pot to be finished off in the usual manner of throwing.

Making pots by this throw-and-coil method

Securing the coil

involves a lot of small squeezing and scraping movements, but Svend Bayer accomplishes this with such professional dexterity that the coils are added in an amazingly short time and the pots grow with apparently minimal effort. It is particularly interesting that the height is achieved by the coiling process and that the throwing is really a polishing and shaping procedure. It is also interesting that he does not score the pots or the coils deeply; the only concession to keying that he makes is to work over the area near the rim with a serrated tool before applying the coil.

The throwing and coiling method was not common in English potteries, if used at all. Around the Mediterranean, though, it has been in use for hundreds of years to make huge terracotta storage jars. At a pottery in Crete, for example, a pair of potters work at a line of six wheels in the open: one turns the wheels by hand, the other coils and throws. The pots they make are huge, the coils they add as thick as arms, and as the pots harden in the sun they work down the row, returning to the first pot just as it is ready to take another coil.

Adding and securing more coils to build up the pot

RIMS

Plant pots traditionally have thick, robust rims. A thick rim can be thrown solid, in which case the clay at the top of the pot must be kept thick from the very start. A collar of clay that looks massive while the form is cylindrical and near the centre of the wheel can be reduced to a narrow band by the time the pot is opened to its full width. In order to prepare for this, it is essential that the rim is fattened at the end of each throwing procedure. It also helps to pull the rim out wide before each lift of the clay.

The other method is rim rolling. This is a dramatic technique, common in the era of country potteries, which displays the plastic properties of clay at their best. The clay wall is kept a uniform thickness from bottom to top at every stage. Then, when the pot has been thrown beyond its final height, the rim is simply rolled over by pressure from the inside. It is rolled right over until it joins up again with the wall. This method produces a robust, beautifully rounded rim. Because the thrower is not trying to balance a thick coil of clay on an ever-thinning wall, this way of throwing is simple, but the wall does need to be thrown considerably higher than the finished pot in order to allow for the loss in height as the rim is rolled.

UPSIDE-DOWN POTS

Certain plant pot shapes benefit by being thrown upside down. The clay is opened out on the wheel head without a base, then as the wall is thrown up, it is also collared in. With a little practice, it is an easy technique to master and is useful for a variety of shapes. Hanging pots made in this way can be finished off with ornamental embellishments. Lids for rhubarb forcers may be completed, knob and all, in one throwing session. Pedestal pots too can be thrown upside down: the pot itself is collared in and a coil of clay or a freshly thrown ring is luted to the pot and thrown into the pedestal. Rims will need cleaning up later, either by turning when leather hard, or by careful fettling with a knife or metal kidney.

In the country potteries of the last century, and even up to the last war, throwing was the central skill and method of production. Simple terracotta flowerpots were made in all sizes from 4cm (1½in) to 76cm (30in) in diameter. The Royal Potteries of Weston-super-Mare employed 50 men in 1874 and produced 20,000 to 30,000 flowerpots per day, mostly on the wheel. The skill and speed of the throwers was similar to that of brick makers, with all movements pared to the minimum and no effort wasted. With a mountain of clay balls at his side and payment based on production, the thrower drove his thumb into the centre of the ball of clay as it hit the

wheel head. No time was wasted centring as his experienced and steady hands mastered the vagaries of the clay, opened the ball with his thumb, then in a continuous movement squeezed the wall of clay between his thumb and first finger as he lifted his hand. The smallest pots had no rim and were wired off and lifed away without stopping the wheel. Larger pots were thrown into the cooling-tower shape, their rims rolled, then their walls straightened.

Although there is little point in trying to emulate these throwers of the pre-industrial era, especially when today machines and vacuum moulding can produce simple pots in quantities that would confound even the most productive of these old throwers, there are lessons to be learned from their methods. The most important is that it does not benefit a pot to spend more time on it than it needs; a pot made directly and economically is taut, fresh, and vibrant.

Today a professional thrower working in terracotta would be expected to throw about a quarter of a ton of clay a day, producing 30 to 45 pots of 9kg (20lb) of clay, or 20 to 30 pots of 13.6kg (30lb), depending on how much decoration was accomplished on the wheel. A thrower going for broke, and with an assistant to prepare the clay and carry away the wares, could convert a ton of clay into pots. Here I will concentrate on quality, not quantity, and leave the machines to count the numbers.

Finished pots

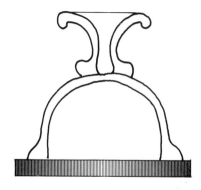

Hanging pot and pedestal pot made upside down

CHAPTER THREE

PRESS MOULDING

Just as throwing exploits the plastic qualities of clay, its ability to flow and bend under pressure, so press moulding exploits clay's ability to take on the shape of the surface against which it is pushed. Clay records the incidental marks of fingers and tools, but this 'memory' can also be used to hold the shape and pattern of any surface that it is pressed against. If the clay is to be removed from the surface against which it is pressed, that surface must be of a material that releases the clay. Typically, moulds are made of plaster of Paris and the clay is released because the plaster draws moisture from the clay, causing it to shrink and therefore pull away. Other materials such as wood or metal may be used, but these must be coated with a releasing medium such as fine sand or oil.

Since press moulding does not primarily make use of the plastic qualities of clay, it follows that a body that is to be used for making press-moulded pots can be quite non-plastic and contain a high proportion of non-clay material, expecially sand or grog of quite chunky grades. This coarse material helps support the clay wall, gives the body a texture or tooth that is pleasant to work with, and reduces the shrinkage. Press moulding, together with other hand-building techniques, releases the potter from the limitations of cylindrical work imposed by the wheel. It also enables him to incorporate more ornate decoration into the pot during the making. Troughs may be made in this way, as can square tubs, face planters, and hexagonal pots. The majority of pots made by press moulding, however, whether heavily ornate or more restrained, remain basically cylindrical.

To make a press mould, it is first necessary to make the master form. This can be hollow or solid, plain or as ornate as you like, the only limitation being that the mould must be able to be lifted away from the clay. It is therefore essential that there are no undercuts that would trap the plaster. The more ornate the pot, the more separate pieces of plaster mould will be needed. A simple pot might be made in a two-piece mould, most pots will require a four-piece mould, while larger and more ornate pots will require a greater number of mould pieces.

Once the master form has been modelled, casting can begin. If a great number of pots are to be made, it will be necessary to make block and case moulds from which working moulds can then be made. The life of a working mould is not indefinite and detail is soon worn by coarse clay. If only a limited number of pots are to be made, the working moulds can be made straight off the master.

Plaster of Paris comes in various grades. The standard potter's plaster, as used in slip casting, is very absorbent but also very soft. Press moulds have to endure quite harsh abuse and are better made from stronger plaster. Such plasters are less absorbent and usually the clay shape will have to stay in the mould for some time while it hardens up.

(Overleaf) Turning and removing a mould from a large pressed frog

Moulds for large forms may be made in the usual way, pouring liquid plaster against sections of the work entirely cottled off from each other by sheets of thin plastic or aluminium. Moulds made in this way are neat, with a smooth outer surface, but may be unduly heavy. Another method is to pour the plaster against a cottled section of the pot, making sure that the surface is covered by smooth, soft plaster. As the plaster hardens, handfuls are slapped on top of the first layer, building up a wall of sufficient but not unnecessary thickness. This process is far easier if a section of the pot has been modelled horizontally within a wooden 'cradle' rather than trying to cast up a free-standing pot.

Jim Keeling: large pressed terracotta pot

Courtyard Pottery: The Four Seasons. *Press-moulded terracotta*

Camilla Lawson: press-moulded planter. Stoneware

John Huggins: face planter. Terracotta

Compton Pottery: small press-moulded plant pot. Early twentieth century

Simon Hulbert: pressed and thrown pedestal pot. Terracotta

Simon Hulbert: pedestal urn. Terracotta

Press moulding was a standard technique employed by many of the country potteries of the last century for making decorative terracotta plant pots, or vases as they were commonly called. As a general rule, pots between 4cm (1½in) and 45cm (18in) in diameter were thrown on the wheel, while larger, more decorative pots were press moulded. Apart from the fact that pot and decoration are completed together in a single operation, the method enables substantial pots to be made without having to lift and work with a single, heavy mass of clay. A further advantage is that although press moulding requires skill, it is not of the same calibre as that required by a thrower. Creative skill is required to imagine and execute the master form, while production requires skills of a different order.

At Whichford Pottery I watched one of Jim Keeling's assistants, Nick Holloway, pressing a 33cm (13in) high garland terracotta plant pot. He uses the same clay as is used for throwing and in the same condition – soft and easily worked. With the clay in this state, it responds easily to being beaten and it picks up well the detail of the moulds.

The four pieces of the mould are first assembled and secured with a rope tightened like a tourniquet. It has no base and is assembled directly onto a wooden bat. Any areas of the mould that have been damaged or where bubbles have occurred in the plaster are filled in with clay. These areas and the base are then dusted with a fired powdered clay to ensure good release from the mould. This dust is sifted in place through an old sock to ensure a light distribution of just the finest dust.

A thick coil of clay is placed in the rim that surrounds the base and is pressed against the plaster, first with knuckles to ensure the clay surface is hard up against the plaster, and then with fingers to smooth the surface of the clay. Three coils of clay follow until the base rim is fully loaded and the clay has been beaten across the base of the pot. Any excess clay above the base rim is peeled away with a

Stephen Dixon: press-moulded lion. Terracotta

finger, leaving a clean surface against which the next slug will lie.

Nick Holloway then prepares a flat slab of clay and places it against the lower part of the mould wall. This is then beaten with a clenched fist to spread and thin the clay. The area where this clay and the base clay meet is given particular attention, with the top clay beaten well into the clay below. Again, any excess at the upper limit of this slab is peeled away with a finger to leave the next (decorative) band clear of scraps of clay, and also to enable the thickness of the wall to be judged. Five further slabs are then added and beaten into place to complete the lower section of the pot. Particular care is taken at the areas where slabs meet to ensure that the slabs do not remain distinct, and that the clay is thoroughly mixed. If Nick wants to check the thickness of the clay wall, he can use a pin, but mostly he knows from experience how far his slab of clay will spread to give him a uniform thickness of approximately 1cm (⅜in).

It is now time to build the upper wall, including the decorative frieze. This is done in the same way, a flat slab being placed over the first area of decoration, beaten into place and trimmed back where the upper rim begins. Care is taken not only that the edges of the slabs mix thoroughly, but also that the clay is punched sufficiently to enter into all the detail of the decoration. Again, another five slabs complete the upper part of the pot.

The thick rim at the top of the pot is then

Adding a slab of clay

Forming the upper wall

Beating the surface

Removing the mould

filled in two stages. A thick roll of clay is fed into the mould and punched firmly in place with the knuckles. A further three coils complete the first layer of the rim. This clay is then smoothed, first with the finger tips and then with the side of the index finger, every smoothing swipe also giving added pressure to ensure the clay is tight up against the mould wall. A thick coil is then rolled and squeezed onto the surface of the earlier coils in a rhythmic twisting action in order to build up a thicker section. This extra clay is then knuckled and smoothed as in earlier operations and the excess removed.

The mould is now full, but not quite finished. Nick goes over the whole surface, beating it with the palm of his hands, partly to smooth, partly to add extra pressure. The more the clay is beaten and paddled, the stronger the joins will be and the smoother the outer surface. The pressing is completed by scraping the base around the bottom edge with a finger to remove excess clay and to add definition to the form, and a drainage hole is cut out with a tin of a suitable diameter. The entire surface is then cleaned with a scraper in upward strokes from the base to beyond the rim. This removes finger marks and gives the pot a clean finish.

The filled mould is then put aside for the clay to harden off. With a pot of this size the mould can usually be removed after about two hours. Fettling the seams between mould sections and around the upper rim is best done as soon as the pot can be handled without distorting. Creases that have occurred between or within the various slabs are sponged away with a few vigorous strokes, but creases within areas of decoration take more careful elimination. Surface creases are a valued charateristic in handmade bricks and in the trade are referred to as 'smiles'. Creases on the surface of a hand-pressed pot, however, are not generally appreciated and are regarded by the buyers of pots as indicating structural weaknesses, though this is not the case.

Press moulding this pot takes Nick Holloway about 45 minutes. Preparation of the coils and slabs, the punching, knuckling, and smoothing are executed with a steady rhythm typical of an experienced maker. He knows just how much clay he needs for each section, how much pressure he must apply and how thick the finished wall will be. He uses as much energy as the work requires, but wastes none.

Larger pots than this may be press moulded. The technique is the same but the work will take longer, with just one or two pots made in a day. A press moulder who worked at Compton Pottery in Surrey between the wars remembers that as a young lad he was employed to press pots whose moulds were so tall that when he leaned over the top of them and reached to the bottom he needed a candle in there to see what he was doing. Wooden paddles of various shapes can be used to beat the clay and these are best covered with hessian to prevent them sticking as they dampen. It is much harder, however, to judge the thickness of clay when using a tool or to make those constant adjustments of pressure necessitated by the vagaries of clay. No tools are as suitable or versatile as hands.

Flowerpot making was traditionally paid by piece rate, a set price for each pot made, the total tallied at the end of each working day. With press-moulded work payment was still by piece rate but, in Sussex at least, the pots were counted at the kiln door during packing. This convention developed because weaknesses and poor workmanship in the construction of a press-moulded pot, rather than simply in its appearance, often does not show until the later stages of drying. Unless the pot is well made, with clay that is in good condition, cracks are likely to occur at the joins between slabs and in areas that are over-thick or over-thin.

(Overleaf) Stephen Dixon: trough. Terracotta

CHAPTER FOUR

MACHINE-ASSISTED PRODUCTION

Individual makers and small workshops generally have neither the wish nor the money to commission machines to make their pots. What joy can there be in spending hours minding a machine that produces identical clones by the thousand, where clay is simply a unit of material in a plastic bag, and the product a figure in a ledger book?

Machines can, however, save physical exhaustion and can be used creatively to help make pots. Few potters would dismiss the benefits of a pugmill, especially if they are preparing a ton and more of clay each week. Machines are good to employ when they feed the maker, rather than when the maker feeds them.

Colin Kellam uses a hydraulic ram press to extrude sections of clay which are then assembled into pots. The variety of shapes he can produce with just square section extrusions is surprising. A particularly magnificent planter is assembled from eight lengths of square section approximately 45cm (18in) long. These are cut in half lengthwise and assembled on a wide slab base. Further extrusions are added for the top rim and for

legs at the bottom. Colin also extrudes shaped sections, a pair of which are assembled into attractive planters. By incorporating extruded slabs between the two ends, extended trough-like planters are made.

Successful extrusion demands a clay that is quite stiff, and problems do arise in trying to prepare a clay with a sufficiently low water content. Clay particles bond well when there is ample water present, but Colin finds the moisture content needs to be kept down to about 14 per cent for satisfactory extrusions. Clay that is pugged as stiffly as this is likely to come out of the pug laminated; the blades cut up and mix the clay, but when it is pushed back together in the tapering nozzle, the clay is too stiff to join up as a single homogeneous mass.

Errington Reay and Company at Bardon Mill used to produce extruded salt-glazed drainpipes, but now the clay and the machines have been adapted to produce salt-glazed plant pots. In an unusual partnership their pots are part machine-made, part handmade.

A thrown disc of clay on a wooden bat is

offered up to the open end of a vertical extruding machine. A cylinder is then extruded directly onto the clay disc which is supported on a counterweight system; as the pipe is extruded, so the support for the disc and bat slides down. The clay pipe is extruded to the length required and wired off, then pipe and disc are placed on a potter's wheel. With minimal effort the base of the cylinder is secured, inside and out, to the clay disc. The pipe, which is now a pot, is given shape by applying pressure on the inner wall as the potter's hand is drawn up from the base. The top is finished off by shaping a suitable rim.

Plant pots of many sizes are made by this technique, the limiting factor being the ability of the thrower's arm to reach inside to the base. While this is not throwing in the full sense, it is a technique that enables pots of a substantial size to be made without back-breaking effort.

Pugmills may be used for extruding shaped sections, although it will be found that the arrangement of the blades often causes the clay shape to extrude in a slight arc. In my workshop we have extruded sections for assembling into troughs, but the bigger we have made them, the more they want to bend. It would appear that large shapes are better extruded through large wad boxes or presses where the pressure is applied evenly across the mass of the clay. Colin Kellam's small hydraulic ram press operates at a pressure of 99.7–113.9kPa (35–40 tons psi), his larger press at 31.3–62.6kPa (11–22 tons psi).

While I have not found much satisfaction in making extruded pots, there is a very wide area here where machines can be used creatively and the pieces they make assembled with imagination.

Colin Kellam: extruded and assembled plant pots. Stoneware

CHAPTER FIVE

HANDBUILDING

Handbuilding techniques include a wide variety of making methods, especially pinching, slabbing, and coiling. All of these methods are employed by various people making pots for plants, but coiling lends itself particularly to the production of large pots for the garden. Although coiled pots may be made to massive dimensions, the potter is handling only relatively small amounts of clay at a time, rather than dealing with a single, large mass as in throwing.

Of the various methods of making covered in this book, coiling is the slowest. It is rarely suitable for the production of repeated shapes. Wheel-thrown pots are made in minutes, press-moulded pots in hours, but coiled pots usually take days or even weeks. It is this slowness of production, however, that is one of coiling's greatest attractions. The maker, the medium, and the model are in intimate contact for extended periods, the maker both willing a form and responding to the demands of the clay. Ideas may be started that prove unacceptable as the shape develops, and unimagined solutions result from this three-way conversation. The shape

Martha Allen: Adam and Eve. *Stoneware*

Ursula Ströh-Rubens: plant pot group. Raku

of a coiled pot grows bit by bit, changing and evolving as coils are built up or scraped away.

Monica Young and Jenifer Jones both make coiled pots for gardens. Monica Young's monumental forms are very much hollow pot shapes with a base, belly, and open top, but developed on such a scale and with such sculptural sensitivity that they are unlikely to be planted up. Working with craft crank clay, she builds her pieces over a long period, up to eight weeks. Starting with crude walls about 4cm (1½in) thick she develops her idea of the shape. As the shape resolves itself, she scrapes clay away, refining the form and defining edges. Her work often incorporates folds like those of hanging fabric, though the sense of suggested movement is balanced by

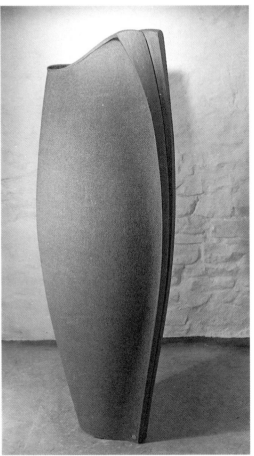

Monica Young: garden pot. Stoneware. Height 152cm (60in)

Jane Norbury: trough. Terracotta

Monica Young: garden pot. Stoneware.
Height 152cm (60in)

Jenifer Jones: urn. Stoneware. Height 66cm (26in)

poise and serenity. She pays particular attention to neat graceful edges, their crisp lines flowing along the swelling form of the pot, their smooth planes contrasting with the lightly textured surface of the mass.

Monica coils her pots on trolleys and uses a fork lift to manoeuvre her 1.5m (5ft) high pieces into the kiln. She fires them up to 1300°C (2372°F)) in a reducing atmosphere to vitrify the clay and minimize its ability to absorb moisture.

Jenifer Jones's coiled pots bridge the space between functional garden pots and sculptural forms. They could be planted up, but rarely are. They are large in dimension but even larger in presence. They are dark and still, generous but restrained. With a bronze-black finish, her stoneware pots often involve a tension between swelling forms, straight lines, and flat planes, their rims and lugs finished with sharp, almost chiselled edges. The coarsely textured surfaces of her pots are decorated with straight incised lines in a fine grid or bold geometric pattern.

Jenifer uses a mixture of crank and red clays and fires to 1260°C (2300°F). She works on three or four pots at a time, taking about three or four weeks from start to finish. The lower coils of her pots may be up to 5cm (2in) in diameter, ready to support the weight of the growing pot. Most coils, however, are about 2.5cm (1in) in diameter and these are squeezed to gain extra height after being securely joined to the growing wall. The oxide pigment is brushed onto the pots after a biscuit firing in order not to distort the clear lines of the decoration when the clay is raw.

In coiling large pots for the garden it is essential that the coils are well and truly joined together. Scoring the surfaces to be joined and the use of sticky slurry helps, but the important thing is that clay from each coil is pushed well into the adjacent coil so that a thorough mixing of the clay occurs. As the form grows it is important that the lower walls are sufficiently sturdy to support the increasing weight of clay. This will usually involve leaving the partially made pot to harden off while taking care that the top rim remains in a soft workable state.

While every effort is made to keep a coil pot uniform and balanced as it is built, it is possible to go back over the shape once it is complete. Using serrated or smooth metal kidneys, the shape and surface can be cleaned up and any unevenness scraped away. Decoration may be modelled on the pot as it is being coiled or the surface treatment may be left until the form is finished.

(Overleaf left) Jenifer Jones: garden pot. Stoneware. Height 63cm (25in)

(Overleaf right) Mariette Voke: garden pot. Stoneware. Height 66cm (26in)

CHAPTER SIX

DESIGN AND DECORATION

SHAPE

Pots for plants may be purely functional or they may aspire well beyond the restrictions of utility. The shape and proportions of purely functional pots, such as the traditional horticultural ware produced in vast quantities for the expanding nurseries at the turn of the century, were dictated by the job they had to do, combined with the most economic shape to produce. The standard sloping-sided flowerpot shape made in numerous sizes from 4cm (1½in) to 76cm (30in) in diameter was, and remains, ideal for plants. Stable on the ground or greenhouse staging, plants could easily be potted on from one sized pot to the next as they grew simply by upturning the pot and dropping out the plant and potting compost. As for production, the shape was easy to make and stacked economically, both for firing and for carriage to the nurseries. Plain pots, half pots, and seed pans were the epitome of economic functionalism, though

John Huggins: watering set. Stoneware

horticultural ware expanded to cover long toms (taller and thinner than pots), rhubarb forcers, herb barrels, crocus pots, and the like. In such ware the basic principle observed was that the pots served the plants.

Today most studio potters aim to produce pots that fulfil more than basic function. This may simply involve making pots with care and by hand in a world where plastics and machines dominate. The simple handmade plant pot is so obviously more appropriate and at home in a garden setting than smooth-surfaced, hard-edged machined pots. Other potters add ornament, combining the function of a basic plant pot with attractive decoration. A few potters produce pots for a garden setting that have less to do with function and more to do with sculpture. In some cases, the pot is more important as an ornament than as a container for plants. Rather than the pot serving the plants, the plants serve the pot.

Tangularium, salt-glazed plant pot designed by Guy Booth, manufactured by Errington Reay

All plant pots should have drainage holes and be wide enough at the base to be stable out of doors in a high wind, bearing in mind that a plant might well increase the height of a pot by up to four times. Apart from that, the range of shapes and decorations that may be suitable for plants is unlimited. Look around and see what odd containers have been brought into commission for planting: from enamelled teapots to china toilets, painted tin cans to cast iron drainpipes and eggcups to wheelbarrows.

As a general rule, a good pot will not detract from the beauty of the plants it contains. The pot and the plants should complement each other to pleasing or even striking effect. This dictates that the form or decoration of the pot should not be too loud or extravagant otherwise the pot will draw attention away from the plants it contains. However, most plants die back in winter, losing their blooms and even their foliage. A good pot will then have to stand alone as an attractive feature in the garden and so must have sufficient presence to provide interest and satisfaction throughout the long winter months. A poor or mean pot will irritate and a pot that is too ornate or loud will quickly bore and have to be hidden behind the garden shed.

Pots shaped to imitate or echo plant forms, such as an opening bud or tulip shape, might be expected to work well in a garden. This is rarely the case. Shapes that owe more to architectural influences, incorporating more straight lines than exaggerated curves, work better. Plant shapes and patterns are infinitely variable, and these patterns change not only with the seasons but with the changing light in the course of each day. A pot is a static artefact and acts best as a foil to the plant world. A garden pot, like a house, is something made by man, and while it should not stand out as a blemish, neither should it blend invisibly with its surroundings.

Svend Bayer: plant pot. Stoneware

(Overleaf) John Huggins: teapot planter. Terracotta. Height 35cm (14in)

SIZE

A feature common to most garden pots is their size. They are not intended for window sills or sideboards and, unlike domestic wares, are often seen at a distance, at the end of a path or across a lawn. If a pot is large and heavy it follows that any handles or lugs must be sufficiently big and robust to be practical. But size is relative: a 60cm (2ft) high pot may look large next to an eggcup, but put it by a tall building or massive oak and it shrinks into insignificance. This indicates the importance of siting, but the same principle can also be used to encourage a sense of size. Non-functional lugs, handles, spouts, etc. can emphasize the size of a pot by being deliberately undersized.

COLOUR AND TEXTURE

Many plant pots, both terracotta and stoneware, rely simply on the colour and texture of the clay for their appeal. Glazed plant pots are rare. It is one of the attractions of plant pots that any decoration, whether by indenting into or building onto the clay surface, is part and parcel of the fabric of the pot itself. Unlike a layer of glaze, the pot and the decoration are inseparable.

DECORATION ON THE WHEEL

Some decorations may be executed while the pot is freshly thrown and still on the wheel.

PIECRUST

Rope effect, or piecrust, is a traditional decoration that can look good if boldly done. A ridge of clay is left on the wall of the pot during throwing, which should be neatened above and below with a rib for emphasis. The ridge is turned into piecrust by repeatedly pressing the edge of the index finger against the ridge. If the finger is pressed in vertically and then twisted slightly, the rope pattern should develop an attractive flow. This decoration should be quite tight under the rim or it will look as if it is slipping down the pot. Sometimes it is easier, especially on wide pots, to add a separate coil of clay for the piecrust, rather than throwing a ridge. As long as any slippery slurry is removed from the surface of the fresh pot, the coil can be added as soon as the pot is thrown or it can be added the following day when the pot has hardened up a little. If the pot is thrown with a rolled-over rim, it is possible to roll over more than is needed for the rim and to develop a ridge out of the excess.

SCALLOPS

Scalloped rims are an attractive alternative to the tradional thick rims. The pot wall is thrown to an even thickness right up to the rim, which is then flared outwards at the end of the throwing. Scalloping is done immediately the pot has been thrown and involves the same technique as stroking a lip for a jug.

Support the outer wall of the rim with the thumb and second finger of the left hand and stroke the clay in between with the wet index finger of the right hand. Stroke it backwards and forwards, applying slight pressure until the scallop is sufficiently pronounced. Spin the wheel slightly and repeat again until the complete rim is fully scalloped. Only a little experience is needed to space the scallops evenly round the entire rim; the last one may have to be slightly larger or smaller to complete the circle. It is a good idea to ensure that the rim is fairly thick for a scalloped edge, or it will look weak and fragile.

(Overleaf) John Huggins: Distressed, *plant pot with white inlay. Height 53cm (21in)*

LINES AND GROOVES

Horizontal lines, engraved into the spinning clay, can bring a simple pot to life or be used to emphasize the various areas of a pot. A single or double line engraved near the bottom and another near the top can be used to suggest the neck, belly, and foot of a pot, especially if the form is quite round. Alternatively, lines can be used to divide the pot into bands, some of which may then be decorated. Grooves may be cut with a tool or more boldly by simply applying finger pressure.

KNOTTED STRING AND ROULETTES

The surface of a freshly thrown pot can be enlivened by combing with a serrated tool, either with long, flowing waves or small, busy vibrations. A more attractive finish can be achieved by rolling a length of knotted string along the surface. Different knots will produce different patterns. The lightly indented surface contrasts well with other areas left plain.

A roulette made of plaster or, preferably, fired clay can also be used to indent a simple decoration into the clay. If the roulette is able to revolve on a wire fixed into a handle, it can simply be held against the freshly thrown pot as the wheel turns. The roulette should be kept in a tub of water during use to prevent it drying and sticking to the pot.

MOULDS

Carved moulds, again either plaster or fired clay, can be held against the fresh pot and the clay wall pushed into the mould from the inside. The moulds must be saturated to prevent them sticking to the pot, and equal pressure applied both inside and outside the pot to avoid distorting the form. With a little experience the clay can be pushed into the mould with sufficient finger pressure to pick up all the detail. The clay must be strong enough to hold its shape during this process or it will collapse. Any irregularities can be made good immediately afterwards by spinning the wheel and trueing up the rim. It is important for this type of decoration that the pot wall is fairly thick or a hole will develop where the clay is stretched.

LATER DECORATION

If a pot can be decorated on the wheel it saves a good deal of time and effort, especially if large quantities are being made.

Decorating with a plaster block

Decorating with a roulette

Many decorative techniques, however, require the clay to have firmed up a little. It is best to finish pots off as soon as they have developed sufficient firmness to be handled without undue distortion, especially if additions of clay are being made to the pot. As the pot gets harder, it will be increasingly difficult to model on other clay satisfactorily. Sandy clays quickly lose their flexibility and will split if handled forcibly.

ROULETTES AND MOULDS

Roulette decoration can be done at the soft leather stage and will give a more sharply defined image than when done on the wheel. I roulette the rain drops to my *Sun and Rain* pots at this stage, as the detail is too fine to be done when the clay is wet and slippery. Pressing the clay wall into carved plaster or clay block moulds can also be done at this stage for the same reasons. If the decoration is bold or extensive it is best done when the clay has firmed up slightly, but if the surface of the pot goes hard it will not want to be pushed into the mould and will tear.

SPRIGS

Sprigs should be applied to pots at the leather-hard stage. The softer the pot clay, the better the bond of the sprig will be. If the surface has gone rather hard it will be necessary to score the pot wall and smear it with slurry paste before applying the sprig. Sprigs offer the opportunity of very bold relief decoration, but they have the inherent

weakness that the sprig may pull away from the pot wall during either the drying or firing. Pressing the clay of the pot wall into a plaster block does not carry this risk.

HANDLES AND TRELLISES

Handles and lugs may be applied to pots at the leather-hard stage, as can extrusions. Trellised pots, also called lattice or basket-weave pots, are decorated by applying strips of thin extrusions diagonally across the pot surface. Before applying such extrusions it is a good idea to mark out the spaces between strips on the bat, or to mark the pot with a pair of callipers. Traditionally such pots have attractively grooved cylindrical handles applied standing up from the rim, which is rusticated by being lightly beaten with a grooved piece of wood such as a butter pat. Trellising is an attractive decoration for plant pots and, if executed boldly, can add a monumental three-dimensional quality to the pot surface.

Stephen Morgan: trellised pot. Terracotta

(Overleaf): Sussex terracotta: sgraffito plant pots

MODELLED SHAPES

Coils, or other additions of clay, may be applied and modelled onto leather-hard pots. Undulating ridges may be applied to enliven a shape, or more formal panels developed to break up simple surfaces. A smooth surface can be transformed into a vigorous landscape of ridges and knolls. These could be developed into bridges and hill-top settlements with modelled dwellings hanging precariously on the pot walls or scattered around the rim. Or they might be developed into the surfacing humps of an underwater monster, whose torso rears up as it approaches the rim. A face could be modelled on the pot, or a lizard caught sunning itself.

The inside of a pot, especially a shallow bowl, may also be modelled. Still leaving enough room for small plants such as cacti, landscapes or buildings can be modelled into the pot. Buildings, bridges, paved areas, and ponds can all be incorporated to provide an attractive, self-contained mini-environment or secret garden. Once modelling starts, the possibilities are endless.

SLIP DECORATION

Slips may be applied to leather-hard surfaces in a variety of ways. Pots may be given a wash of thin watery slip that will settle in any decorative detail or simply break up the uniformity of a plain pot. A thicker coat may be painted on which, when dry, may be scratched or carved through to reveal the original body. This technique, sgraffito, can be striking when an entire pot is decorated with a well-planned design. It does not work so well for just a band of decoration.

Clive Bowen decorates many of his large earthenware planters with slip. He paints the entire surface with a large, flat paintbrush, while slowly turning the pot on a banding wheel. He paints the rim and the band at the top with white slip, and the rest he paints with a black slip. When these base slips are sufficiently dry, he decorates them with thicker slips applied with slip trailers. The decoration is quickly executed with lines and loops trailed with unfussy flourishes from bottom to top. When the pots are thoroughly dry they are raw glazed on the outside, the glaze being painted on with a wide, flat brush.

Inlaid slip decoration is a technique that works well with any clay body and at any temperature. Its effect is achieved by developing a crisply defined pattern and by the lively contrast between the slip and body colours. The pattern is engraved when the pot is leather-hard. The incised grooves are then filled, either by brushing on coats of thick slip, or by smearing on slip of a paste-like consistency. In order not to trap air bubbles in the incised lines, it is best to paint or paste the slip along the lines, not across them. When the pot and the slip are sufficiently hard, or even thoroughly dry, the excess slip is scraped back with a metal kidney to reveal the decoration. Although white slip is most commonly used, other colours may also be effective.

(Overleaf) Clive Bowen decorating with slips

Clive Bowen: glazed plant pot. Terracotta

Peter Stoodley: garden pot. Stoneware inlaid with vitreous slip

OXIDES

Bone-dry pots may be given a wash of oxide, usually black iron oxide or possibly manganese dioxide. This will blacken the surface and may give a slight metallic sheen. If it is then sponged off again, the oxides will linger in recessed areas to highlight decoration and contrast with unblackened plain surfaces.

Henry Pim: plant pot and stand. Stoneware. Height 75cm (30in)

GLAZE DECORATION

Glazed plant pots can look very dramatic in a garden or patio, and they often suit an interior situation better than unglazed pots. They come into their own, however, in conservatories. where they can be appreciated in an environment that is usually stylish, warm, and with plenty of natural or artificial light.

The entire repertoire of glazing and decorating techniques is available for use with plant pots. Because of the scale of plant pots generally, certain techniques become unwieldy. It is impractical, for instance, to dip large pots in huge vats of glaze; if no spraying equipment is available, it is best to stand a whirler in a wide plastic bowl and pour jugfuls of glaze over the pot as it is slowly rotated.

(Overleaf) Marion Brandis: trough. Terracotta

For economic reasons it is advisable to raw glaze large pots if this is possible. The glaze should contain as much body clay as possible, perhaps with additions of bentonite, and be applied at the dry or leather-hard stage, depending on the nature of the body. Raw glazing at the dry stage is much easier than having to keep watching pots for the right leather-hard moment before the rims start changing colour, but it will work only if the body is very open or sandy. With large pots it is sometimes advisable to wipe a damp sponge over the inside before glazing the outside in order to balance stresses caused by the absorption of water.

USING KILN ATMOSPHERE

Kiln atmosphere may be used to decorate the surface of a pot. Salt, or less environmentally damaging soda (salt produces harmful hydrochloric acid), firings at high temperature can provide a range of attractive surfaces from a light sheen to heavy orange peel effect. Salt-glazed pots which incorporate oxide-bearing slips look especially handsome on paved areas or against stone walls.

Terracotta is traditionally fired in a clean oxidizing atmosphere to produce pots of a bright uniform colour. Tones vary from light to dark depending on whether they are from a cooler or hotter part of the kiln. Other atmospheres may be employed, however, to produce various effects. Controlling kiln atmospheres is not easy, results are unpredicatable, and repetition unlikely. At lower temperatures salting is uncommon, but terracotta or other lighter-firing earthenware clays may be salted at around 1100°C (2012°F). In order to make the salt flux, it should be mixed with borax before being thrown into the kiln.

Blue brick firings can echo a technique that used to be familiar, though always precarious, in the brick industry. By introducing a heavily reducing atmosphere in the kiln at its top temperature, the red iron oxide that gives terracotta its typical red colour can be converted to black iron oxide. This atmosphere should be maintained for at least an hour and may need to be maintained during cooling to prevent re-oxidation. The effects will usually be a bluish- or brownish-black and this may be accompanied by a slight sheen if the oxides have started fluxing.

Introducing dense smoke into the kiln at lower temperatures may produce pots that are carbon black. With the damper fully in and all holes and cracks clammed up, excess fuel can be introduced to develop dense smoke. Wood, inner tubes, pitch, etc. can be thrown in to encourage smoking, and cans of water may also be thrown in to build up pressure by converting to steam and so encourage greater penetration of the carbon into the pots. Some pots may turn out a disappointing grey, but a successful firing will produce pots that are pure jet black.

(Overleaf) John Huggins: salt-glazed plant pots

CHAPTER SEVEN

DRYING AND FIRING

Drying time for pots will depend on their size, the nature of the clay, and the prevailing heat and humidity. Space in any workshop is always limited, and it is important that pots dry as quickly as possible so that they may be fired and shelf space made available for the next batch.

The optimum arrangement is when pots are made, dried, and fired at the same rate, so that production is not held up due to lack of shelf space, nor firings postponed due to ware not being dry. A cycle like this might rely on the kiln being fired in order to dry the next kiln load, and would require assistants to pack and unpack kilns while the next batch of pots is being made. Arrangements like this are quite efficient, but do impose their own rhythms on production.

Small workshops often adapt to less efficient arrangements, in which kilns wait empty until pots are made and ready to fire. It clearly makes sense to be using waste heat from a firing to dry the next kiln load, rather than let the heat escape and then pay for fuel to heat the workshop and dry the pots. In order to utilize this waste heat, it is important

that the kiln's capacity is not so large that firings are too intermittent. To use the waste heat just once each week, the kiln's capacity should be about equal to the capacity of a week's work.

If it is thought economic to have waste heat every day, then having one or two smaller kilns, each with the capacity of a day's production, is a reasonable arrangement. With the low thermal mass kilns now available and computer programming commonplace, firing kilns need not be the marathon task it once was. The cost of setting up such kiln facilities, with their regular use of waste heat, can be set against the cost of heating a workshop day and night through the cold winter months.

Each ton of plastic clay has to yield approximately 225l (50 gal) of water during drying. The brick and ceramic industries have pursued ever more efficient means of production. Studio potters have been glad to benefit from advances in kiln materials, but have been generally slow to adopt more efficient methods of drying. Without mass production rapid drying is not so important,

but when potters in Stoke-on-Trent say their work is ready for the kiln 20 minutes after making, and one's own pots still have not changed colour after three weeks on the shelves, there is probably something to be learned.

To facilitate even drying it is important to get pots turned over onto their rims and onto slatted shelves as soon as possible. Large pots are best kept away from sources of heat until they have hardened up sufficiently, then moved nearer the heat as they begin to dry.

Drying depends as much on humidity as on heat. When the weather is wet and the air fully charged with moisture, pots will take longer to dry even with heaters on. I find I can dry large pots more successfully in the winter than I can in the summer, even though I have the wood stove roaring in the day and a gas fan heater on at night. The reason is that the air is already damp and the pots dry out more evenly than during the fierce dry heat of summer. Pots are prone to cracking if they dry too fast and too unevenly.

If intermittent heat, as used in most workshops, is drying pots satisfactorily and

Martha Allen: wall fountain. Stoneware

John Huggins: Sun and Rain *planter. Terracotta. Height 35cm (14in)*

in a short enough time, then that system is good enough. If, however, it is taking too long or pots are being lost due to uneven drying, then setting up a drying room governed by a dehumidifier might be a good idea. Dehumidifiers can be programmed to regulate both the ambient humidity and temperature. This means that moisture can be drawn evenly from the whole surface of the pot, not just exposed parts such as rims, and drying can be considerably faster than in an uncontrolled situation. In my own workshop the smallest pots can be dried in just one or two days, 9–13.5kg (20–30lb) pots in one week, and 18kg (40lb) pots in two to three weeks. Two-part pots of approximately 27kg (60lb) of clay usually take three to four weeks. Larger, thicker pieces, such as our large frog, need considerably longer; surface colour-change is no guarantee that all available moisture has been drawn out. A very thick large piece of work may need two to three months to be ready for firing.

Any type of kiln is suitable for firing plant pots, though again, since garden pots are large, suitable kilns are generally large too. Large pots, especially if they are thick-walled, need carefully controlled firing. Low-mass kiln bricks and ceramic fibres do not absorb heat in the same way as heavier materials and this is very good for keeping firing costs down. However, care must be taken to ensure that large pots do not heat up too fast during the firing, or stresses will occur and cause cracking. This potential risk will be increased

if temperatures vary greatly between the top and bottom of a large pot. Rapid cooling is equally risky and may have to be offset by firing downwards as well as on the way up. A small kiln firing just one or two large pots may be prone to dunting during cooling. A larger kiln will contain more pots and therefore more mass to retain heat.

Electric kilns have a static atmosphere, and the heat from the elements is transferred to the pots mostly by radiation. They are rarely more than 60cm (24in) wide. Live flame kilns work mostly by convection but also by radiation, producing a more even heat distribution which is more suitable for firing large pots.

The most important part of the firing cycle is the initial pre-heating. Also called tanning, dewatering, or water smoking, this period of the firing ensures that all available moisture, or physically combined water, is slowly driven off. Brickyards and some potters pre-heat their kilns for two days. I pre-heat my 5.6 cu. m (200 cu. ft) oil kiln with gas overnight for 12–15 hours and hope the temperature will be between 120°C (248°F) and 150°C (302°F) when I arrive in the morning. Smaller pots, under 9kg (20lb), I might fire in the electric kiln, programmed to rise to 120°C (248°F) in four hours. If the pots rise much above 100°C (212°F) before all water is driven out, the water will turn to steam within the fabric of the pots and either shatter them or cause a mass of cracks to develop as it forces its way out.

The remainder of the firing need not be so slow, although it is a good idea to be particularly careful until above 400°C (752°F). As the pots work their way through dull red to orange, so they are able to accommodate a faster rise in temperature. I programme the electric kiln to fire the middle temperatures at 55°C (131°F), then from 450°C (842°F) upwards at 75°C (167°F), giving a total firing time up to 1070°C (1958°F) of 18 hours. The large oil kiln may take twice that time, due partly to a mixture of caution and convenience.

Front-loading kilns, however large, are a pain in the back. Invariably you have to keep your back bent while lifting pots into place, and the arched roof limits the use of available space. Kilns should be able to be packed without the hindrance of the kiln sides and roof. Top hat kilns, rolling trolley kilns, or rolling hood kilns are just as simple to make and will allow much easier and more economic packing.

Packing a kiln with unglazed terracotta plant pots is a joy compared with packing glazed work. You do not have to ensure that pots do not touch and become stuck together, or check that kiln dust or other debris does not fall into a glazed dish. It is just as important, however, to get as much work in each firing as possible.

In theory, you don't need kiln shelves and can simply stack the pots from the floor to the top of the kiln. If a large number of identical pots are being fired this is sometimes

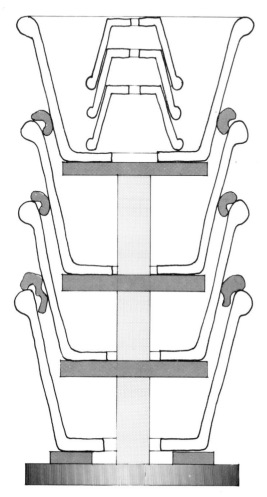

Stack of large pots in kiln, supported on central column of props

Rolling hood kiln, approx. 5.6cu.m (200cu.ft)

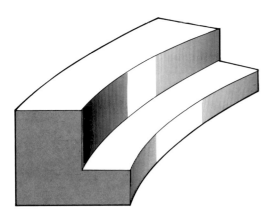

Pan ring – useful for stacking shallow bowl shapes

possible, but invariably pots of various shapes require firing together and a certain amount of shelving becomes necessary.

A variety of techniques can be employed to fit as many pots in the packing space as possible. Traditional flowerpot shapes can be stacked in columns, the height of which depends on the size and weight of the pots. The smallest pots I would stack as high as there is room for, but I am cautious with bigger pots that have taken more time to throw and decorate: 9kg (20lb) pots are stacked four or five high, 13.5kg (30lb) pots three or four high. More bulbous pots will not stack inside each other and are best stacked rim to rim and base to base. Smaller pots can be put inside the hollow forms. The bottom pot in such a column has to support

quite a weight, and only trial and error will show when the limit has been passed. In a column of five 35.5cm (14in) high pots each weighing 20.5kg (45lb) when freshly thrown, the bottom pot supports a little over 50kg (110lb) of dry clay.

Pan rings may be useful to support columns of bowl-shaped pots. The pan rings, made of fired sagger clay, are arranged in a circle with gaps between each brick. The bowl is placed with its rim on the ledge of the bricks. Further circles of brick provide ledges for further bowls until a column several feet high has been built.

Pots which will sit inside each other, but whose weight makes it risky to do so, may be stacked using a central pillar to take the weight. The central drainage hole may be thrown large enough to accommodate a prop, or, at the risk of spoiling a good pot, a large disc can be cut out of the base to be fired separately. Standing the bottom pot on bricks, a shelf prop is placed centrally through the drainage hole and a piece of broken shelf or a circular bat balanced on top of that. The second pot is now placed on the balancing shelf and adjusted until it is stable. Pieces of broken pots, fired or not, or small bowl shapes are then slipped between the inner and outer pot to lock the second pot into place. More pots may be added by repeating the process, and as long as the props are in line and the pots well chocked with smaller pots or shards, a column many pots high remains very stable.

My rule of thumb for stacking is that if pots stack safely before firing, they will be safely stacked at the end of the firing, so long as the firing schedule is unhurried. But disasters do occur and the bigger the gamble in stacking, the more dramatic will be the disaster.

CHAPTER EIGHT

WEATHER RESISTANCE

Garden pots must withstand the vicissitudes of the weather and the rigours of life in the garden. The winds will blow them, driving rain pelt them, cruel frosts freeze them, burning sun parch them, and playing children knock them. The garden may be a tranquil haven in the cool of a summer evening, but time and tide will turn and it is no place for a lightweight or poorly made pot.

A good outdoor pot must be sufficiently heavy and with a wide enough base that it will not easily be dislodged by wind or a careless knock. The walls must be thick enough that the pot will withstand a degree of handling, knocking, or even knocking over. You cannot expect a pot to survive being knocked over onto paving, but it should remain intact if knocked onto earth or grass. There is no merit in seeing how many pots can be made from a weight of clay if they all come out as thin as teacups.

John Huggins: Sun and Rain *planters*

All outdoor pots should have drainage holes, either in the base or cut at the bottom of the side. Plants can suffer from drowning as well as parching, and it is essential that surplus water is able to drain away from the roots and potting compost.

Frost is the severest critic of outdoor pots and will easily separate the good pots from the poor pots. Terracotta has been burdened with a bad name since the war, owing to the weak pots imported from Mediterranean countries, especially Spain. These pots are generally fired too low and disintegrate at the sight of a snowflake. I claim my terracotta pots are frost proof. It is not uncommon for a customer to come into my workshop and say, 'I bought some of your pots last year. You told me they were frost proof.' 'That's right', I reply, suppressing a rising panic as I think she might be about to produce the remains of a shattered pot from her bag. 'Well, you are right! I arranged them in a group with some other pots I had bought from a garden centre. Yours survived the winter, but several of the others flaked, a few cracked and some completely disintegrated.'

A terracotta pot's ability to withstand frost is based on a series of factors. There is no magic ingredient, no single additive that will give a pot charmed protection. Features inherent in every stage of the potting process – the material used, the method of making, and the firing – combine to produce a pot that will withstand even heavy frosts. Clay for making good plant pots must be soft.

Clay particles that are well lubricated with water slide by each other easily, developing the material's plasticity, and, as the the water evaporates, the particles come into tight proximity. Handfuls of soft clay easily mix and dry to a strong mass, but clay that is stiff does not mix well, nor does it make a strong mass when dry. Joining distinct masses of clay, as in making two-part pots, coiling, press moulding, etc., is satisfactory as long as the clay is soft, but all potters know how troublesome it is to join two pieces of clay that have gone stiff. The join may be made to work, but it will always remain a source of weakness if the material from the two masses has not been properly mixed and married.

Machines, of course, cannot manage with soft, sticky clay. They have to use clay with a much lower water content than we would like to throw with. Stiff clays are likely to have inherent weaknesses in them when they come from the pugmill, the extruded mass of clay actually being more or less concentric layers of clay that have not thoroughly bonded. When clay like this is pressed by machines into pot shapes, the clay in the walls becomes a series of layers or laminations instead of a single homogenous mass. When these pots are exposed to the stresses of weathering their weaknesses are quickly exposed and the laminations spring apart. Typically, large thin sections or shells with sharp edges spring off the wall or rim of the pot. Often after a frost attack the distinct layers within the broken pot are clearly visible.

Terracotta clay for plant pots should be tempered with sand, not grog. Grogs are fired fireclays ground to various sizes ranging from dust to chunky granules. However, they are not fired to their maturing temperatures and so remain quite porous. As terracotta is not fired to a sufficiently high temperature to reduce the grog's porosity, it acts in the fired pot as a host of tiny sponges ready to absorb moisture. If these pieces of grog are saturated and the pot freezes, the water in them will expand and create a multitude of tiny points of tension sufficient to cause cracking and, in severe cases, even crumbling. Stoneware pots can safely use grogs since their high firing will mature the grog as well as the clay.

Sand, of course, is non-porous and will not conserve water. It is easily available in various grades to add feel or tooth to the clay while helping to reduce its shrinkage. Sands may well be contaminated with lime, however, which does absorb moisture, and therefore need to be tested before use. One local sand I tested was so full of tiny lime particles that after four weeks out of the kiln the test pot had completely disintegrated, due to the lime dots expanding with absorbed atmospheric moisture. Washed sands can be purchased, but they are more expensive.

For a potter with the appropriate grinding machinery, pitchers are the ideal tempering material. Pitchers are the body clay fired and ground and have the advantage over grogs of

Courtyard Pottery: bird house. Terracotta

maturing at the same temperature as the clay into which they have been mixed. Wasters from the kiln and other damaged pots can all be turned into pitchers, providing the grinding machinery is available.

Just as machines build weaknesses into the pots they press, so throwers build strength into the pots they throw. A thrown pot has a spiral structure built into the wall as a result of the way the clay is lifted on the spinning wheel during the throwing process. Like a spring this structure is able to accommodate a certain degree of tension.

All clays develop their maximum strength at different temperatures. While it is true that most Spanish plant pots are fired too low to develop a reasonable strength, it is not correct to say that terracotta must be fired to 1060°C (1940°F) for example, to develop its strength. Some surface clays will mature below 1000°C (1832°F), while other terracottas must go above 1100°C (2012°F) to develop any real strength. What is important is that the clay is sufficiently fired to develop its maximum strength and to reduce its moisture absorption to a fairly low level. A good terracotta pot will absorb moisture, and this is one of its advantages over non-porous materials, but it must not soak up water like a sponge.

Commercially prepared terracottas based on Etruria Marls often have a high percentage of fire clays in them. This gives the body a wide maturing range and they are not easily over-fired – in fact they are often classified in catalogues as stoneware/earthenware. Highly plastic terracottas, however, usually have a narrow maturing range. They vitrify soon after the body has become quite dense and, if the temperature rises further, will quickly soften and deform. With most downdraught kilns, temperature and heat distribution are fairly easy to control, so not many pots should be lost through over-firing. To develop a clay's maximum strength, however, it is important that pots are not under-fired. If pots at the bottom of a kiln tend to be under-fired, an hour's soaking at the top temperature will probably help. With live flame kilns, opening the damper further will draw heat to the bottom of the kiln. Any pots that are drawn from the kiln under-fired should be put back in the kiln for a further firing.

It is a mistake to think of unglazed terracotta garden pots as biscuit ware. Some professional stoneware potters have been known to remark, 'I make a few terracotta plant pots for fun. It's so simple. Things never go wrong.' Biscuit firings by definition imply a second, usually higher, firing and aim to produce ware that is sufficiently strong to be handled without breaking, while suitably porous to suck up and hold glaze slop. Firing unglazed terracotta plant pots has quite a different purpose: to develop maximum strength and low to minimum porosity.

The clay, how it is made up, and the firing are all factors that work towards or away from the production of a frost-resistant pot.

The most important factor, however, is drainage. Water must be able to soak away from plant pots before freezing weather sets in. No sensible car owner neglects to add antifreeze to his radiator water at the onset of winter, and no plant pot owner should forget to raise pots off the ground, either by pushing pebbles underneath or by raising the pots onto pot supports. The most telling illustration of the importance of proper drainage as a defence against frost damage I have seen was a large handthrown terracotta pot that had to be 30 years old at least standing on a brick patio. The pot was able to drain freely and was in fine form. The bricks, however, were mortared onto a concrete base and were unable to drain. Consquently the bricks were in a dreadful condition, having flaked and cracked very badly.

Makers of handmade bricks use very sandy open-textured clay and usually fire them to well below their vitrification temperatures. They say that clay is a naturally occurring material and can stand up to all weathers because the openness of the texture means that the bricks absorb water easily, but they give it up easily too, by drainage or evaporation. Machined clay, they argue, absorbs water but because of the density of the material is more prone to suffering frost damage because it does not let the water go easily. Some bricks do suffer from spalling, flaking, or crumbling of the surface, due to frost penetration. Where this occurs it will

John Huggins: Ivy pot. Terracotta. Height 45cm (18in)

usually be found that the wall is saturated and cannot drain properly, that the clay mix was rough and contained hard pieces that had not been properly mixed in, or that the bricks were under-fired. Often just certain bricks in a wall suffer from spalling and were those that had been too low fired and should have been returned to the kiln. The standard test for gauging the frost resistance of a brick is to saturate it in water then freeze it to a particular temperature, $-10°C$ ($14°F$) for example. Let it thaw, then repeat the sequence a number of times, simulating the effect of heavy rain followed by hard frosts. A good handmade pot should stand up to this test as well as any brick.

Shape is also an important factor, both for terracotta and for vitrified stoneware. Sodden compost in a traditional straight sloping-sided flowerpot can expand upwards unrestricted during freezing conditions. Garden pots with narrow necks and deeply rounded sides allow no room for wet compost to expand during freezing and are likely to shatter around the neck or the belly during severe weather. Pots with exaggerated curves, such as Ali Baba-shape planters, are best potted up by sitting a traditional pot inside the neck.

A terracotta plant pot, handthrown with a well-prepared, soft, highly plastic clay, fired to a temperature approaching vitrification and able to drain thoroughly, will not suffer spalling or lamination. If the shape is right it should not crack either, but a pot in a garden can easily be knocked by a lawn mower or

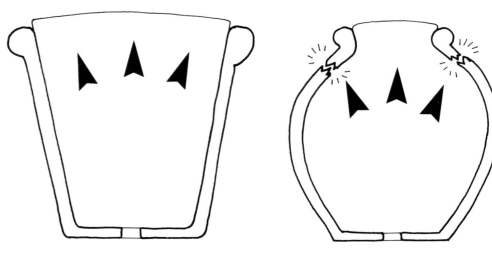

The effects of freezing on open-topped and narrow-necked pots

wheelbarrow and the damage not become apparent until exposed by frost.

It has been standard practice for older gardeners to empty pots before the winter, or move them into a shed. It is good to encourage such care, though a well-made pot will survive so long as it can drain thoroughly. If all the rumours about terracotta breaking in the winter were true, we would have to rebuild our brick houses each summer. As it is, we have fine examples of terracotta brick architecture that have survived for centuries and look better and richer as the years pass. It is the mortar between the bricks that is more likely to need

replacing. There are terracotta flower pots in use today at Kew Gardens, London, which were made at the Royal Potteries in Weston-super-Mare before the turn of the century.

CHAPTER NINE

PLANTS FOR POTS

The range of plants suitable for growing in pots is extensive. Colourful displays may be composed of annual bedding plants that will last for a few months. Small trees, shrubs, and perennials may provide less dazzling displays but still give interest over a longer term. Box bushes or bay trees, clipped to shape, add a formal touch to any garden or patio.

Before plants are chosen there are certain considerations that need to be given thought. Is the pot or group of pots going to be incidental within the overall design of the garden or is it to be a focal point? Should the plants add a splash of colour or is mass and shape more important in a particular location? Will the plants or the pot be the main feature? Will the planting be perennial or seasonal?

Several pots together may work well as a group, especially if the shapes and materials are similar. A group of bulbous pots or of straight-sided pots will work well, but if mixed together will not be as successful. Grouping three pots of the same design but of varying heights will usually make an attractive display. Beware of collecting numerous little pots that will each require careful attention and watering. A single large pot will be more rewarding than many small ones.

The needs of the plant should also be considered. Is there enough room for root growth? Is the location suitably sunny, or does a particular plant, such as a fern, prefer a shady spot? Does the plant require a particular type of soil, either alkaline or acid? Pot planting, of course, has the advantage over open gardening in that there is no problem in providing particular composts for particular plants, such as lime-free compost for rhododendrons.

When preparing a pot for planting it is important to provide adequate drainage. If water cannot soak away from stem and root growth there is a real possibility that rot will set in. The drainage hole should be covered but not blocked by a curved shard or large stone, and the bottom third of the pot filled with pebbles, stones, shards, etc., through which excess water can drain away from the growing medium.

The growing medium, or compost, may be varied according to the needs of the particular plant, but a good all-purpose compost is the widely available John Innes Number 2. A home-produced version can be made by mixing two parts by volume of

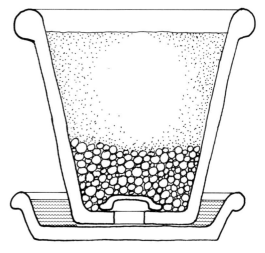

Potting up

sieved loam (garden soil in good heart) with one part peat and one part coarse sand. Nutrients can be added according to suppliers' recommendations. Garden soil should never be used on its own as it dries and quickly compacts too tightly.

Pots do dry out quickly in the summer and even if the sun is not out a warm wind will quickly draw away moisture. Pots must be watered regularly in dry periods, often every day and sometimes twice a day. Standing a pot in a drainage saucer will help a terracotta pot as the water will percolate up through the slightly porous wall. The planting compost will not provide sufficient nutrients to maintain good growth for more than three or four weeks. After this pot plants will require supplementary feeding. The simplest way is with a general purpose liquid fertilizer.

When choosing plants to harmonize with a pot it is a good idea to estimate how big the plants will grow. The proportion of pot size to plant growth is best kept to one part pot to two or three parts plant, though, conversely, tall thin pots often work well with short or stocky plants, such as polyanthus or dianthus, or trailing plants such as trailing nasturtium. While large pots will support a large plant or group of plants, they sometimes look better filled with small plants. The range of plants suitable for growing in pots, whether annuals, perennials, or shrubs, is so extensive that those mentioned here must serve just as examples.

Spring-flowering bulbs are always a pleasure, heralding the advent of spring. They require little attention and are easily grown. Planted in the autumn and kept in a dark cupboard or under black polythene until the bullet-like shoots are an inch or so above the compost, they indicate hope of spring even in the depths of winter. Crocuses, planted either in pots or through the holes of crocus/herb pots, provide an early touch of colour. Dwarf bulbs are the most practical and attractive varieties for pots as they are not so easily damaged by the wind as their taller-growing relatives. Dwarf daffodils and narcissi are a delight to see in pots, their colourful heads shaking in the spring breeze. Flowering slightly later, miniature tulips, especially the strong red variety, make a bold display emphatically proclaiming that winter is dead.

Summer plantings may make use of any of the numerous bedding plants to provide pots of colour. These may be planted alone, mixed, or combined with hardy perennials. Plants of a single type such as small violas, dwarf nasturtiums, marigolds, or convolvulus look very effective, their shapes and colours appearing clearly without the distractions of more varied plantings. When bringing groups of plants together in a single pot, a general principle is to include something tall, something trailing, and something colourful. Within these varying levels, flower and foliage colour can be chosen to contrast with each other. In this way the colours and patterns of each plant remain distinct while contributing to the overall effect of the massed plants.

Geraniums are the classic pot plant for summer colour. They have a long flowering period, revel in sunny positions, and will withstand a degree of dryness. There are numerous varieties: two that are always excellent in pots are 'Dolly Varden', with variegated foliage in cream, rosy red, and green with flame-red flowers, and the stocky 'Red Fox' with dark brown/green foliage and bursts of small brilliant red petals.

For dramatic effect the sword-like leaves of the cordyline are always eye-catching. This plant is equally impressive whether grown on its own in a pot or adding distinction to a mixed planting. The trumpet-shaped flowers, often striped, of petunias can be relied on to provide colour in pots, as can the more compact forms of begonias. Begonias, especially semperflorens, are remarkable for providing masses of small flowers, and these endure when most summer flowers are beginning to die back. Chrysanthemums of many varieties will provide colourful and scented displays right through the autumn months.

Even in the depth of winter, plant pots with dwarf conifers will provide points of interest on a patio. Though belonging to the least dramatic or colourful class of plants, they do hold their own in pots when all the annuals are dead and even the perennials have lost their leaves. Their interest can be developed by bringing together species of

John Huggins: pedestal pot. Terracotta

contrasting shapes and colours. Crocus bulbs buried beneath the stone chippings around the conifers will soon send up their signals of hope that winter days are numbered.

In many respects, grouped alpines make the most successful year-round pot plants. Though never providing the eye-catching colour or dimensions of shrubs or annuals, these hardy little fighters practically thrive on neglect. They hang on through successive droughts, deluges, and snow drifts, their cushions and clusters slowing multiplying and merging with each other. From time to time they will throw up clusters of elegant starry flowers. Alpines do not like to be waterlogged so their growing medium must contain sharp sand to allow good drainage. They do not require a deep soil, and a coating of grit or small pebbles on top of the compost is an attractive foil and keeps dampness away from plant growth. Many species can be put together in a small space, their varied shapes and colours composing a garden in miniature. The saxifrages and sempervivums are the most easily grown. The plants can be left to colonize all available space and will then start creeping over the rim of their pot. In a restricted space many of them push themselves into attractive hummocks.

Ivies are ideal year-round pot plants. In a mixed planting they are useful as trailing plants, while alone they may be trained up supports of sticks or a column of chicken wire filled with sphagnum moss and grown into spectacular pyramids or pillars of

Alpine plants in bloom

cascading leaves. Varieties with cleanly defined leaf shapes are the most successful, while the variegated ivies look particularly good in shady situations.

Choosing plants for pots can be an exciting challenge. Common plants and standard combinations can be relied on to provide abundant growth and plenty of colour. The range of possibilities is endless, however, and successful combinations of plants and pots will be discovered only through taking risks and experimenting.

CHAPTER TEN

DECORATIVE BRICKS, TILES AND OTHER ORNAMENTS

The clay used for making handmade bricks is very similar to that used for thrown plant pots except that it is much softer, in the state known in the brick industry as wet mud. It is likely to contain grit and pebbles that would be too coarse for potting. Soft clay for bricks is not pugged but is usually passed through roller grinders or a pan mill to crush hard clay and stones to a small size. Water is added and the clay thoroughly mixed with revolving blades. Openers such as sand may be added, while some works add breeze or coal dust to assist with firing. When the clay is ready it is almost of a pouring consistency and is tipped onto or by the work benches.

Making plain bricks is hard work, a repetitive slog to accumulate 700–1000 bricks a day. Decorative specials employ the same basic technique, but because they are more intricate and command a higher price the pace of work is more relaxed.

Bulmer Brick and Tile Company in Suffolk produces an extensive range of handmade bricks on a site that has been a clayworks since the mid-fifteenth century. When I visited, I watched one of the women workers

produce tapered bricks with a simple decoration in high relief. These bricks are laid on end to form circular chimney stacks with a lattice decoration.

The walls of the box moulds used for brick making are usually made of soft wood. The heavily carved face is traditionally made of hard wood, usually beech, though soft wood is now often used. Fine sand is used as the releasing agent and this also gives the bricks their typical granular surface. Where this rough finish is inappropriate, moulds can be brushed with oil.

Bulmer Brick and Tile Company: decorative bricks

Making decorative bricks at Bulmer Brick and Tile Company. Carved face of the mould

Assembling the mould

Dropping the clot into the mould

Cutting away excess clay

Inverting the mould

Removing the mould

For making the tapered chimney bricks the mould is first assembled. It is a simple box mould but has a tapering insert on either side secured in place with metal rods passed through the end walls. The assembled mould is filled with sand by being pushed into the open-fronted sand box, then inverted to empty the excess. Because the mould walls are damp through constant use the sand sticks easily.

The clot, or warp, of clay for making the brick is prepared by scooping the required amount of clay from the supply, using joined hands as a blade to slice through the mass of soft clay. The clay is rolled in a bed of sand and is formed into the appropriate shape to drop into the mould. The clot is usually wedge-shaped so that when the thin end hits the bottom of the mould it will spread without trapping air. Dry fine sand is usually used, but if a brick is required with exaggerated creasing, damp sand can be used.

The clot is dropped from a height into the mould. The filled mould is then lifted and given a sharp bang by dropping it on a firm surface. In this way the clay should fill the mould completely and travel into every detail of the decoration. Excess clay is cut free with a harp and lifted away. The exposed surface is smoothed with quick strokes of a rolling pin kept in a bucket of water then lightly coated with sand.

The mould is then lifted and lightly dropped on each side to ensure that the clay is released from the mould walls. The two wooden inserts are removed, a piece of slate or wood is placed over the exposed surface, and the mould inverted. The mould is then lifted away leaving the freshly pressed brick glistening through its lightly sanded surface. Bricks like this take about 7kg (15lb) of clay while large coping bricks can take as much as 55kg (1cwt) at a time.

Decorative bricks and tiles carrying high-relief moulding can have many uses in a garden. Apart from single bricks having ornamental value in their own right they can be built into attractive garden walls, raised beds, or even assembled into monumental pots.

The garden, considered as another room of the house, can be furnished in much the same way as any other room. The garden is a room to be lived in and, as such, may be furnished with seats to sit on, tables to eat at or put things on, pictures to look at, and ornaments to consider. Many of these furnishings can be made of clay. Seats and stools made of high-fired stoneware can be attractive and useful in a garden. Though hardly lightweight they will endure all weathers and improve rather than deteriorate with age.

Chris Lewis: garden seat. Stoneware

(Overleaf) Compton Pottery: pressed terracotta seats. Early twentieth century

Earl Hyde: pagoda. Stoneware

Sarah Walton: birdbath. Salt-glazed stoneware. 74 × 60 × 11cm (30 × 24 × 4½in) (Overleaf) Sarah Shirley, Architectural Ceramics: Sun *fountain*

Gwen Heeney: garden shelf. Terracotta

It is always worthwhile incorporating water into the composition of a garden. Whether this is in the form of a pond, a fountain, or simply a bird bath, the sound and surface of water can enrich a garden. Still water reflects the patterns of moving clouds and the play of sunlight; rippled water displays rhythmic patterns changing to the play of the wind; the sound of pouring water is both tranquil and refreshing. Elaborate fountains several tiers high, or mask tiles spouting water, are well within the production possibilities of even small pottery workshops. Thrown, press-moulded, coiled, or modelled – the challenge of producing water features opens many possibilities.

Just as pictures are hung on walls inside the house, so tiles and plaques can be used to decorate walls around the house and garden. From functional name and number plates hung by the front door to decorative architectural embellishments sited on walls or around the garden and colourful tile panels depicting a story, the opportunities for design and expression in clay are limitless.

Jane Moore: The Tiger *wall plaque*

Statuary, ranging from the simply unmentionable to the impressively sculptural, deserves a place in any garden. Pieces can be sited to form a point of focal interest in a formal garden or they may provide incidental interest mixed with plants, pots, or other garden furniture. Although stone, and, more recently, reconstituted stone, has traditionally been the favoured medium for garden statuary, terracotta figures were part of the standard production lines in the larger country potteries in Victorian times.

Today there are new possibilities for designing and making statuary appropriate to contemporary buildings and gardens. Animals, figures, mythical beasts, and putti, whether modelled individually or press-moulded, can make a welcome addition to any garden. Gardenware makers, of both pots and ornaments, should take heed of the past, though without slavishly copying its designs or decoration. Instead they must imaginatively develop styles and decorative vocabularies appropriate to contemporary architecture and garden design.

John Huggins: Sun and Rain *pot. Terracotta. Height 35cm (14in)*

Stephen Dixon: pedestal pot. Terracotta

Stephen Dixon: wall plaque. Terracotta.

SUPPLIERS

CLAYS

Potclays Ltd,
Brick Kiln Lane,
Etruria,
Stoke-on-Trent,
Staffordshire

Spencroft Ceramics,
Spencroft Road,
Holditch Industrial Estate,
Newcastle,
Staffordshire

Valentine Clay Products,
The Slip House,
Birches Head Road,
Hanley,
Stoke-on-Trent,
Staffordshire

C H Branham & Co Ltd,
Roundswell Industrial Estate,
Stickle Path,
Barnstaple,
Devon

These commercial clay suppliers all produce terracotta and other clays that can be used for throwing and handbuilding plant pots. I do not recommend any of them for throwing large pots. That is why I produce my own.

My own blend of clays, 'Real Terracotta', is available in both small and large quantities from my workshop, Courtyard Pottery, Groundwell Farm, Cricklade Road, Swindon, Wiltshire. The original blend gave some potters trouble in the drying due to its high plasticity and shrinkage together with its high sand content. The Mark 2 clay is more tolerant of varying drying conditions.

SAND

Joseph Arnold and Sons Ltd,
Billington Road,
Leighton Buzzard,
Bedfordshire

INDEX

References in italics indicate illustrations

Ali Baba-shape planters 76
Allen, Martha *42, 67*
annuals 7, 77, 78
Architectural Ceramics 87
architectural influences 49–50, 89, 90
ark 11, *12*, 14

ball clays 12, 25
banding wheel 58
Bardon Mill (Errington Reay) 40, *49*
barium carbonate 14
base, of pot 16, 17, *17*, 18, 22, 24–6, 36, 49, 71
basketweave pots 56
bats, throwing 22, 36, 40
bay trees 77
Bayer, Svend 24, *24–8*, *25–7*, 50
beating 18, *18*, *23*, 24–5, 36, *37*, 38
bedding plants 77, 78
begonias 78
bentonite 64

bird baths 86, 89
    house 73
biscuit ware 74
block moulds 55
    plaster 54, 56
blue brick firing 64
blunger 11, *12*, 14
body clay 64, 72
Booth, Guy *49*
borax 64
Bowen, Clive 58, *59*, 60
box bushes 7, 77
    moulds 81–4, *82–3*
Brandis, Marion 63
brick making, historical 9, 11, 29, 64, 66, 74–6
bricks, decorative 81–4, *81–3*
brickyards 11, 68
bulbs 7, 78
Bulmer Brick and Tile Company 81, *81–3*
butter pat *23*, 24, 56

cacti 58
cakes, clay 12–14
callipers 18, 22, 23, 25, 56
carved moulds 54

casting 30–32, *31*
centring 15–16, *17*
chimney bricks 81, 83
    pots 24
chrysanthemums 7, 78
clay 25, 36, 46, 64, 72, 74, 76, 81, 93
    cleaning 11–14
    for moulds 54
    preparation 10–14, *12*, *13*, 25
    throwing 15–29, *17–27*
clot, of clay *82*, 83
coils 58
    piecrust 52
    see also coiling
coiling 25–7, *25–8*, 36, 38, 42–7, *42–7*
collaring, of wall 29
colour, of pots 52
combing 53
commercial clays 10
compost 76, 77–8
Compton Pottery *34*, 38, 85
cone, clay 16, *17*, *17*
conifers 7, 78–80
conservatories 62
cooling 68

cooling-tower shape 16, 18, 29
coping bricks 83
cordyline 78
country potteries 9, 10, 15, 28, 29, *34*, 36, 90
Courtyard Pottery (John Huggins) *32*, 73, 93
cracking 14, 66, 68
'cradle' 32
Crete 27
crocus pots 49, 78
crumbling 74–6
crystals 14

de-airing, of clay 13
decoration 30, 36, 46, 52–65, *53–7*, *59–63*, 65, 81–90, *81–91*
dehumidifiers 68
design 48–52, *48–51*
dewatering 68
Dixon, Stephen *front cover*, 36, 39, *91*
downdraught kilns 74
drainage 74, 77
    holes 16, 18, 38, 49, 70, 72
    saucer 78
drainpipes 40

drying 66–8
    room 68
dunting 68

earthenware 58, 64, 74
electric kilns 68
equipment, clay preparation 11–
    14, *12*, *13*
Errington Reay and Company 40
Etruria Marls 10, 12, 74
evaporation 74
extruding, sections of clay 40, *41*
extrusions 56

face planters 30, *33*
fertilizer 78
fettling 29, 38
filter press 11–14, *13*
firing 68, 72, 76
flaking 74–6
flowerpot, standard shape 19, 48
fountains 67, *87*, 89
freezing 72, 74, 76, *76*
frieze 36
frost 72, 74, 76, *76*
function 48–9

garden centres 9
    furniture 9, 84, *84*, *85*
    shelf *88*
geraniums 7, 78
glazes 52, 58, *60*, 62, 64, 68
grog 10, 14, 25, 30, 72
grooves 53, 58
grouping pots 7, *77*

handbuilding 42–7, *42–5*, *47*
handles 52, 56

hanging pots 29, *29*
heat distribution 74
heaters 66
Heeney, Gwen *88*
herb barrels 49
    pots 10, 78
hexagonal pots 30
history, 9, 11, 15, 24, 27, 28, 29,
    34, 36, 38, 48–9, 52, 64, 76,
    81, 85, 90
Holloway, Nick 36, 38
horticultural ware 48–9, 90
    see also history
Huggins, John *33*, *48*, *51*, *53*,
    65, 67, *71*, *75*, *90*, *93*
Hulbert, Simon *35*
humidity 66
Hyde, Earl *86*
hydraulic ram press 40, *41*

industrial pottery making 10
inlay 53, 58
inside, of pot (modelling) 58
iron oxide 62, 64

jaw crushers 11
joining 23–5, *23*
Jones, Jenifer 44, *45*, *46*, *47*

Keeling, Jim *32*, 36
Kellam, Colin 40, 41, *41*
Kew Gardens 76
keying 27, 46
kidney, metal 29, 46, 58
kilns 46, 66–70, *69*, *70*, 76
    atmosphere 46, 64
    computer programming 66
    downdraught 74

electric 68
    front-loading 68
    live flame 68, 74
    packing 68–70
    rolling hood 69
    shelves 68–70
kneading 16–17
knotted string, decoration 53

lamination 76
lattice pots 56
Lawson, Camilla *33*
Lewis, Chris *84*
lids 29
lifting 18–22, *20*
lime 11, 72
lines 53
location 77
long toms 49
lugs 22, 52, 56

machine-assisted production 40–
    41, *41*, 72, 74
manganese dioxide 62
measuring 18, 22, 23, 24–5
Mediterranean 27, 72
modelled shapes 58
Moore, Jane 89
Morgan, Stephen 56
moulds 30–39, *31–7*, *39*, 54, 55, 84,
    90
    box 81–4, *82–3*

name plates 89
nineteenth century *see* history
Norbury, Jane *44*
nurseries 9, 48

oil kiln 68
opening up, of base 17, *17*
orange peel effect 64
ornament 49, 81–90, *86–91*
over-firing 74
oxides 46, 62, 64

packing, kiln 68–70
paddles 26, 38
pagoda 86
pan grinder 11
    mill 81
    rings 70
panels 58
patios 7, 62, 78
pedestal pots/urns *front cover*, 29,
    29, *35*, *91*
penetrometer 13–14
perennials 77, 78
petunias 78
piecrust 52
pillar, kiln 70
Pim, Henry 62
pinching 23, 24, 42
pitchers 72
plants 7–8, *8*, 48, 49, 72, 77–80, *77*,
    80
planters 30, *33*, 40, *51*, 58, 67, *71*,
    76
plaques, wall 89, *89*
plaster 53, 54, *55*
    block 54, 56
    of Paris 30
plastic pots 9
plasticity, of clay 10, 28, 30, 66, 72,
    74, 76
ponds 89
porosity 74

pre-heating 68
preparation 10–14, *12, 13*
press moulding 30–39, *31–7, 39*, 90
pressing 11–14, *13*, 85
props, kiln 69, 70
pugging 13–14, *13*
pugmill 11, 13, 40, 72
pumps 11–13

raku *43*
ram press, hydraulic 40, 41
rhubarb forcers 24, 29, 49
ribs 16, 22, 23, 24
ridges 52, 58
    throwing 16, 22
rims 16, 18, *21*, 22–6, 28, 29, 36,
    40, 54, 58, 72
    rim rolling 28
    rusticated 56
    scalloped 52
roller mill 11
    grinder 81
root growth 77
rope effect 52
roulettes 53, 55, *55*
Royal Potteries, Weston-super-
    Mare 8, 29, 76

sagger clay 70
salt 11, 64
salt-glaze 40, 45, 49, 64, 65, 86
sand 10, 14, 30, 55, 72, 74, 81, 83
scallops 52
scoring 27, 46, 55
sculpture 46, 49, 90

seats, garden *84, 85*
sections, extruded 40–41
seed pans 48
sgraffito 57, 58
shape 48–50, *48–51*, 76
    modelled 58
shelves, kiln 66, 68–70
    prop 70
Shirley, Sarah 87
shredder plate 13
shrubs 7, 77, 78
sieving 11, 14
siting, of pots 7, 52
size 52
slabs, of clay 36, 37, 40, 42
slip 11–12, 14, 58
    casting 9, 30
    decoration 9, 58, 59
    inlay 58, *61*
    trailing 58
sludge pump *12*
slurry 14, 16, 22, 23, 46, 52, 55
small plants 58
    trees 7, 77
soda 64
soil 77, 78
soluble salts 14
Spain 72, 74
spalling 74–6
sprigs 55–6
stacking, kiln 68–70
statuary 90
Stoke-on-Trent 10, 12, 25, 66
stone 89
stoneware 9, *30, 41, 42, 44, 45*, 46,

*47, 48, 50, 52, 61, 62, 67, 72,
74, 76, 84, 84*, 86
    vitrified 76
Stoodley, Peter *61*
storage jars 27
strength 74
Ströh-Rubens, Ursula *43*
studio potters 49, 66
summer 7, 78
surfaces 58
Surrey, Compton Pottery *34*, 38
Sussex potteries 24, 38
Sussex terracotta 57

tanning 68
temperature, kiln 68, 74, 76
terracotta *front cover*, 9, 29, 32,
    33, 35, 36, 36, 39, 44, 51, 52,
    56, *57*, 60, *63, 64, 67*, 72, *73,
    74, 75, 85, 88, 90, 90, 91*
    clays 10–14, *12, 13*, 93
texture, of pots 52
throwing 15–29, *16–24*, 74
    and coiling 22, 25–7, *25–8*
    and joining 22–5, *23*
    bats 22
    a piecrust ridge 52
    ribs 16, 18, 22, 23, 24
    ridges/rings 16, 22
tiles 84, 89, *84–9*
tooth 14, 25, 30
trees 77
trellises 56, *56*
troughs 30, 39, 40, 41, 44, *63*
trueing, of rim 24, 54

tubs 30
two-part pots 22–7, *23–7*

under-firing 74, 76
upside-down pots 29, *29*
urn *45*

vacuum moulding 29
vacuum pump 13
'vases' 36
Victorian *see* history
vitrification 46, *61*, 74, 76
Voke, Mariette *47*

wall, of pot 9, 18, 22, 25–6, 28, 29,
    37, 54, 55, 56, 71, 72
    plaques 89, *89*
Walton, Sarah 86
ware board 16
wasters 74
water 74, 77, 89
    content, of clay 11, 14, 40, 64,
    66
    smoking 68
    watering plants 77, 78
weather resistance 71–6, 84
Weston-super-Mare, Royal
    Potteries 8, 29, 76
wheel 15–29, 52–4
    banding 58
wheel head 17, 22, 23, 29
Whichford Pottery *32*, 36
winter 2, 49, 76

Young, Monica 44–6, *44, 45*